get crocked

Easy
Slow Cooker
Recipes

Contents

Lemon Poppy Seed Bread pg. 22

Hi friends! Here in my new book, *Get Crocked Easy Slow Cooker Recipes*, I'm sharing tons of simple, delicious recipes that your family is sure to love. Each one is easy to prep and toss in the slow cooker, and hours later you'll open the lid to find a tasty breakfast, dinner, side or dessert ready to go! Some of my new favorites include Bali's Beef & Broccoli (actually, it's my daughter Bali's favorite!) and Caramelized Pineapple with Coconut Ice Cream.

You know I love all my slow cookers—I've already written two cookbooks dedicated to my favorite kitchen tool. It's the easiest way to plan around my busy lifestyle, allowing me to prep a meal whenever I have time for it, then go about my day while the slow cooker does the rest of the work. But for my third cookbook, I wanted to introduce you to another fun and practical way of cooking: Pressure cooking in the Crock-Pot® Express.

We've all been there: You've planned your meals for the week, bought the groceries and maybe even prepped the dish the night before. Then you get to work and realize, "Oh no, I forgot to put dinner in the slow cooker!" This is one of the many reasons why I wanted to write this new cookbook and share my passion for pressure cooking in the Crock-Pot® Express. Yes, I still LOVE slow cooking, but pressure cooking is great for those days when we don't have time to plan, or we get busy and before we know it, it's 5 p.m.

That's why every recipe in this book includes two sets of cooking directions: One for the slow cooker, and one for the Crock-Pot® Express. So no matter what your schedule is like, you're covered to prepare a mouth-watering, home-cooked meal for your family. It's the best of both worlds!

Happy Crocking!

xOxO, Jenn Bare

P.S. If you're new to pressure cooking, don't worry—the learning curve is short, and you'll get the hang of it in no time! Be sure to check out my FAQs before you get started.

Pressure Cooking
Tips & Tricks

Getting Ready to Cook

- Water is key to pressure (FAST) cooking—there must be enough liquid in the recipe or in the bottom of the Crock-Pot® Express and trivet or the dish will burn. See the "burn notice" section of the Crock-Pot® Express user guide for more details.

- Speaking of liquid, because all the liquid is trapped in the pressure cooker, there is less evaporation than other cooking methods (like slow cooking). A good rule of thumb is ¾–1 c. of water when using the "fast" method in the Crock-Pot® Express.

- The FAST cooking time indicated for each recipe is the time it takes to cook and pressure release once the Crock-Pot® Express starts cooking. Note that it can take 10 minutes or longer for the cooker to reach the correct pressure (the timer will countdown).

- Never load the Crock-Pot® Express more than ⅔ full. Any more than that can make a mess when cooking fast! At the same time, having the pot less than ½ full when slow cooking can dry out the meat.

- Some pressure cookers have a "manual" setting. The Crock-Pot® Express does not, so you

PRE-SET TIMES FOR THE CROCK-POT® EXPRESS FUNCTIONS

EXPRESS SETTING FUNCTION	PRE-SET COOKING TIME	ADJUSTABLE RANGE
Beans/Chili	20 minutes High Pressure	5 minutes to 2 hours
Brown/Sauté	30 minutes High Pressure	5 to 30 minutes
Dessert	10 minutes Low Pressure	5 minutes to 2 hours
Meat/Stew	35 minutes High Pressure	15 minutes to 2 hours
Multigrain	40 minutes High Pressure	10 minutes to 2 hours
Poultry	15 minutes High Pressure	15 minutes to 2 hours
Rice/Risotto	12 minutes Low Pressure	6 to 30 minutes
Slow Cook*	4 hours HIGH temperature	30 minutes to 20 hours
Soup	30 minutes High Pressure	5 minutes to 2 hours
Steam	10 minutes	3 minutes to 1 hour
Warm	Keep food warm	30 minutes to 4 hours
Yogurt	8 hours, LOW temperature	6 to 12 hours
SLOW COOKING CAN BE SET TO LOW OR HIGH TEMPERATURE. (NOT A PRESSURE SETTING)		

can select any pressure cooker setting (like the Soup setting) then adjust the time and toggle between High and Low Pressure.

- The Crock-Pot® Express has pre-set buttons for cooking. These are just suggested cooking times and settings. The main thing you need to decide when "fast" cooking is the pressure setting and the cooking time.

- You may notice that the recipes you follow in this book may have a suggested cooking setting that doesn't match up (ex: a dessert recipe cooked on Multigrain setting), and my reason for that is for you to have to press as few buttons as possible. Most times you'll just have to select the Cook setting, slightly adjust the time and press start!

- To adjust cooking time, press the "+" or "-" button until the correct time is displayed, then press start.

- Always make sure the lid is locked into place and steam valve is closed when using a pressure cooking setting.

- Always cook in the removable inner pot or the Crock-Pot® Express. Be careful not to put ingredients in the cooker without the inner pot!

- The inner pot of the Crock-Pot® Express is nonstick, which means it's great for easy clean up, but you also need to be careful not to scratch it. I recommend using wooden or silicone cooking utensils.

- Buy a sling to place between the trivet and the ovenproof dish when using the "pot in pot" cooking method. To make your own sling, take about 2 feet of aluminum foil and fold in third longways. Place the

middle of the foil piece on top of the trivet with the "arms" folded over the sides of the cooking pot. Place the ovenproof dish on top of the sling and fold arms in when placing the lid on the Crock-Pot® Express. Lifting the dish out of the cooker is now easy to do! (The sling can be reused many times.)

Maximizing Flavor

- For best flavor, sauté veggies and brown meats before pressure cooking. To do this, heat oil in the Crock-Pot® Express and use the Sauté setting.

- After searing meat or sautéing veggies, remove ingredients and deglaze the pot with broth or wine. Use a wooden spoon and scrape up any brown bits while deglazing.

- To ensure consistent cooking throughout, do not overlap meat. If you're cutting meat into pieces before cooking, be sure to cut them into uniform size for best results.

- Make a recipe, adjust ingredients to your liking and make it again. Practice makes perfect!

Releasing the Steam

- **QR** = **Quick Release.** A Quick Release means just that; you quickly release all the pressure form the cooker by opening the steam vent. USE CAUTION

when doing this! The steam will be extremely hot and can cause a burn. I always use the end of a wooden spoon to flick open the steam vent.

- **NR** = **Natural Release.** A Natural Release allows the pressure to dissipate naturally. Just keep the steam vent closed after cook time. It will take between 5 and 50 minutes for the pressure to release.

- The float valve is located in the handle and will indicate when the pressure has dropped and the lid can be opened.

Rice and Pasta Guide

- Rice is a breeze in the Crock-Pot® Express! Always use a 1:1 rice to water ratio. (Yes, it seems strange but remember there is less evaporation in the pressure cooker.)

- *Cooking times vary by rice type:*

  Brown Rice 24 minutes High Pressure, 15 minutes Natural Release

  White Rice 3 Minutes High Pressure, 15 minutes Natural Release

  Wild Rice 30 minutes High Pressure, 15 minutes Natural Release

- Need a quick pasta dinner? Noodles are a snap in the Crock-Pot® Express too! Just add 16 oz. uncooked noodles plus 4 c. water to the Crock-Pot® Express. Cook on High Pressure for 5 minutes followed by a quick release. Serve with your favorite pasta sauce.

What's better than waking up to the smell of cinnamon in the morning?

Breakfast

Start your day off right with a hearty first meal.

Add chopped green onions for a bit of extra flavor!

Sausage and White Cheddar Breakfast Casserole

Casseroles are just as delicious in the morning as they are later in the day.

YIELD 8 to 10 portions **I** **SLOW COOK TIME** 8 hours **I** **EXPRESS COOK TIME** 25 minutes

Ingredients

1 lb. sausage
20 oz. frozen hash browns
8 oz. white cheddar cheese, shredded
8 eggs
1.5 c. milk
Salt and pepper, to taste
½ t. ground mustard

NOTE Halve ingredients for Crock-Pot® Express.

Directions

SLOW

1. Brown sausage and place on a paper towel-lined plate to drain.
2. Butter the bottom of slow cooker.
3. Evenly spread hash browns across bottom of the slow cooker. Next, spread sausage over the potatoes. Sprinkle cheese evenly over the sausage.
4. In a medium bowl, combine eggs, milk, salt, pepper and ground mustard. Whisk well.
5. Pour egg mixture over the ingredients.
6. Cover and cook on LOW for 8 hours.

FAST

1. Brown sausage and drain on a paper towel-lined plate.
2. Butter the bottom and sides of a heat-proof insert that will fit inside the Crock-Pot® Express. Combine hash browns, sausage and cheese in the insert.
3. In a medium bowl, combine eggs, milk, salt, pepper and ground mustard. Whisk well. Pour egg mixture over ingredients in insert and stir gently to combine. Cover insert with foil.
4. Pour 12 oz. water in bottom of the Express and place a trivet inside. Place insert on top.
5. Cover with the lid and lock into place. Ensure steam vent is closed. Select Beans/Chili setting (High Pressure) for 25 minutes. Do a quick release of the steam, then carefully open lid and set aside.
6. Using hot pads, carefully lift bowl insert and invert casserole onto a large plate.

Veggie and Egg Casserole

Start your morning with some warm, crumbly casserole. This flavorful dish will fill you up and have you ready to take on whatever the day has in store!

YIELD 8 to 10 portions I **SLOW COOK TIME** 6 to 8 hours I **EXPRESS COOK TIME** 20 minutes

Ingredients

- 4   English muffins
- 1   (14.5-oz.) can diced tomatoes, drained
- ½   onion, diced
- 1   small pkg. sliced mushrooms
- 1   red, yellow or green bell pepper, diced
      Salt and pepper, to taste
- 6   oz. grated Gruyère or Swiss cheese
- 8   eggs
- ¾   c. milk
- 1   t. garlic powder
- 1   T. fresh rosemary, chopped
- 1   T. fresh chives, chopped
- 1   T. fresh thyme, chopped

Directions

SLOW

1. Grease the bottom and sides of a large oval slow cooker.
2. Split English muffins and spread over bottom of slow cooker.
3. Drain diced tomatoes and sprinkle over English muffins. Next, add onions, mushrooms and peppers. Add salt and pepper to taste, then sprinkle cheese over veggies.
4. In a separate bowl, combine eggs, milk, seasonings and more salt and pepper. Pour egg mixture over ingredients in slow cooker. Gently press down to ensure all ingredients are moistened. Cover and cook on LOW for 6 to 8 hours.

FAST

1. Split English muffins and spread over bottom of Crock-Pot® Express.
2. Drain tomatoes and combine with onions, mushrooms and peppers in a small bowl. Add cheese, salt and pepper.
3. In a separate bowl, combine eggs, milk, seasonings and additional salt and pepper.
4. Pour egg mixture over the veggie ingredients and stir. Pour over English muffins. Cover with lid and lock into place.
5. Select Beans/Chili setting (High Pressure) at 20 minutes. Do a quick release of the steam then carefully open lid and set aside.
6. Using hot pads, carefully lift insert and invert casserole onto a large plate.

Sneak some veggies into your diet early in the day!

"Homemade" Cinnamon Rolls

Don't bother setting your alarm. The smell of fresh cinnamon rolls will work much better.

YIELD 10 portions I **SLOW COOK TIME** 3 to 4 hours I
EXPRESS COOK TIME 20 minutes

Ingredients

- 1 loaf frozen bread dough
- ½ stick butter, softened
- 1 T. cinnamon
- 1 c. brown sugar
- ¼ c. heavy cream

FOR GLAZE

- 3 T. heavy cream or milk
- ½ c. powdered sugar

Directions

SLOW

1. Take bread out of the freezer and thaw on greased cookie sheet on countertop.
2. In a small bowl, combine butter, cinnamon and brown sugar.
3. Roll thawed dough out to a large rectangle, about 12 in. x 6 in. Spread sugar mixture over the entire rectangle of dough. Roll dough in a log shape, keeping dough taut. Dip your fingers or a pastry brush into water, moisten the edge slightly and seal shut.
4. Slice into 10 pieces and arrange in a greased 6-quart slow cooker. Cover with a dish towel and let sit for 30 to 60 minutes or until rolls have doubled in size.
5. Pour heavy cream over cinnamon rolls. Cover and cook on LOW for 3 to 4 hours or just until cooked through.
6. Mix cream or milk and powdered sugar to make a glaze. Drizzle glaze over cinnamon rolls before serving.

FAST

1. Follow steps 1–3 of the SLOW recipe.
2. Slice into 10 pieces and arrange in greased ovenproof dish that will fit inside the Crock-Pot® Express. Cover with a dish towel and let sit for 30 to 60 minutes or until rolls have doubled in size.
3. Pour heavy cream over cinnamon rolls. Pour 1 c. water into cooker and place trivet inside. Place insert on top of trivet and cover with a paper towel and foil.
4. Select Dessert setting and switch pressure to HIGH for 20 minutes. Allow natural release for 15 minutes.
5. Mix cream or milk and powdered sugar to make a glaze. Drizzle glaze over cinnamon rolls before serving.

Spinach and Cheese Frittata

This simple, tasty and healthy recipe will take the stress out of breakfast.

YIELD 6 portions I **SLOW COOK TIME** 1 hour to 1 hour 30 minutes I **EXPRESS COOK TIME** 15 minutes

Ingredients

1   T. extra virgin olive oil

½   c. diced onion

3   eggs

3   egg whites

2   T. milk (I use almond or coconut milk)

1   c. mozzarella cheese, shredded, divided

1   garlic clove

¼   tsp. white pepper

1   c. chopped fresh baby spinach, stems removed

1   tomato, diced

    Salt and pepper, to taste

Directions

SLOW

1. Sauté onion in oil over medium heat for about 4 to 5 minutes or until tender.
2. Lightly spray the inside of the slow cooker with nonstick cooking spray.
3. Whisk eggs, egg whites and milk. Stir in onion, ¾ cup of cheese and remaining ingredients, and pour into slow cooker. Top with the rest of cheese.
4. Cover and cook on LOW for 1 hour to 1 hour 30 minutes, or until eggs are set.
5. Test with a knife inserted in the center. If it comes out clean, the frittata is done!

FAST

1. Heat oil on sautè setting and cook onions until soft, about 3 minutes.
2. Meanwhile, butter the bottom and sides of a ovenproof dish that fits inside the cooker. Transfer onions to insert. Combine remaining ingredients in a bowl and pour over onions.
3. Place a trivet in cooker and pour 1 c. water on top. Cover dish with foil and place on top of trivet.
4. Cover with lid and secure. Ensure steam vent is closed. Select Beans/Chili setting (High Pressure) at 15 minutes.
5. Do a quick release of the steam then carefully open lid and test the frittata. If knife comes out clean, use hot pads to carefully remove the insert. Let cool 3 minutes before serving.

Clean Out

If you have any leftover vegetables that you've been desperately trying to get out of your fridge or freezer, now is the perfect time to use them. Just make sure to sauté the other vegetables with the onion; sometimes certain vegetables, like mushrooms and tomatoes, will water down your eggs if they aren't sautéed beforehand.

you can also sub out the brown rice for quinoa, if desired!

Breakfast
Burritos

Add a dash of flavor to the beginning of your day with this delectable dish!

YIELD 10 to 12 portions **I** **SLOW COOK TIME** 4 to 5 hours **I**
EXPRESS COOK TIME 7 minutes

Ingredients

1   (15-oz.) can black beans
(with liquid)
1   (10-oz.) can diced tomatoes &
green chiles (with liquid)
1   c. brown rice, uncooked
2   c. vegetable broth
1   c. frozen corn
3   green onions, sliced
Juice of 1 lime
1   t. ground cumin
1   t. chili powder
½   t. smoked paprika
1   T. minced garlic
12   eggs
1   c. milk
Salt and pepper, to taste
12   flour tortillas

GARNISH WITH

Shredded cheese

Lime juice

Fresh cilantro

Salsa

Lettuce

Avocado

NOTE Use white rice for Crock-Pot® Express.

Directions

SLOW

1. Combine beans, tomatoes, rice, broth, vegetables and seasonings in a 4.5-quart slow cooker.
2. Stir well and cover. Cook on LOW for 4 hours.
3. Whisk eggs and milk and scramble in skillet. Add salt and pepper, to taste.
4. Warm tortillas between two slightly dampened paper towels in the microwave.
5. Spoon bean filling into a warm tortilla. Top with egg, and garnish with desired toppings.

FAST

1. Pour 1 c. water in the bottom of the cooker. Add trivet and place a greased heat-proof insert on top.
2. Combine all ingredients except tortillas and toppings into insert and cover with foil.
3. Cover with lid and lock. Cook on the Rice setting (Low Pressure) for 7 minutes. Quick release steam and remove lid.
4. Stir ingredients and spoon into tortillas. Top with garnishes.

Lemon Poppy Seed Bread

Save some room for a slice of this delicious treat! It's so sweet that it'll make you feel like you're eating dessert for breakfast.

YIELD 12 portions **I** **SLOW COOK TIME** 1 hour 30 minutes to 2 hours **I** **EXPRESS COOK TIME** 55 minutes

Ingredients

- 2 c. flour, all-purpose
- ¼ c. poppy seeds
- 1 T. baking powder
- ½ t. salt
- 1 c. sugar
- 3 eggs
- ½ c. vegetable oil
- ½ c. plain Greek yogurt
  or sour cream
- ¼ c. milk
- 1 t. lemon zest
- ¼ c. lemon juice, fresh
- 1 t. vanilla extract

ICING (OPTIONAL)

- 2 c. powdered sugar
- ½ t. lemon zest
  Lemon juice and/or milk

Directions

SLOW

1. Spray slow cooker with nonstick cooking spray.
2. Combine flour, poppy seeds, baking powder and salt in a large bowl. Set aside.
3. Whisk sugar, eggs, oil, yogurt, milk, lemon zest, lemon juice and vanilla extract until sugar dissolves in a medium bowl.
4. Mix sugar mixture with flour mixture all at once. Stir until combined (mixture will be lumpy). Spoon batter into prepared slow cooker or a bread pan/dish that will fit inside your cooking vessel.
5. Cover and cook on HIGH for 1 hour 30 minutes to 2 hours or until top appears set.
6. Turn cooker off. Remove lid carefully so condensation from lid does not drip onto bread. Cover the top of the cooker completely with paper towels; placing the lid on top. Cool for 10 to 15 minutes.
7. Run a knife around edges of slow cooker; remove bread and set on countertop to cool. Cool completely on a wire rack or plate.
8. If using icing, combine powdered sugar and lemon zest in a bowl. Add 1 teaspoon liquid at a time, stirring after each addition, until desired consistency is reached.
9. Drizzle bread with lemon icing, if desired.

FAST

1. Grease a loaf pan with cooking spray.
2. Combine flour, poppy seeds, baking powder and salt in a large bowl. Set aside.
3. In a medium bowl, whisk together sugar, eggs, oil, yogurt, milk, lemon zest, lemon juice and vanilla extract.
4. Add sugar mixture to flour mixture. Stir until just combined (mixture will be lumpy). Spoon batter into prepared bread pan.
5. Cover the pan with a paper towel and then foil. Seal the lid and ensure steam vent is closed. Cook on Multigrain setting for 55 minutes. Naturally release steam for 10 minutes.
6. Carefully remove the lid. Remove the bread from the cooker and cool for 15 minutes.
7. Drizzle bread with lemon icing, if desired.

Peaches & Cream Oatmeal

Switch out your bland, boring oatmeal for this sweet alternative.

YIELD 8 portions **I** **SLOW COOK TIME** 6 to 8 hours **I**
EXPRESS COOK TIME 6 minutes

Ingredients

- 4 c. old fashioned oats
- 3.5 c. water
- 2 T. butter
- 3.5 c. vanilla almond milk
- ⅓ c. brown sugar, plus more for garnish
- 2 c. sliced peaches (fresh or frozen)
- ½ tsp. salt, or to taste
- 2 t. cinnamon
- 2 c. half-and-half

Directions

SLOW

1. Add all ingredients except half-and-half to the slow cooker.
2. Stir well and place cover on pot.
3. Cover and cook on LOW for 6 hours. (Note: If making these overnight, be sure to use the digital slow cooker that will switch to WARM after 6 hours.)
4. Carefully remove lid and stir.
5. Serve in bowls and top with half-and-half and additional brown sugar.

FAST

1. Add all ingredients except half-and-half to the Crock-Pot® Express.
2. Stir well and place cover on pot. Ensure cover is locked and steam vent is closed.
3. Cook on Multigrain setting for 6 minutes.
4. Let pot release steam for 10 minutes then carefully remove lid and stir.
5. Serve in bowls and top with half-and-half and additional brown sugar, if desired.

For a different sweet touch, you can switch out the brown sugar topping for honey!

Hash Brown Casserole

Get all of your breakfast favorites in one dish. This casserole includes all of the makings of a hearty feast: eggs, bacon and hash browns.

YIELD 10 portions **I** **SLOW COOK TIME** 8 hours **I**
EXPRESS COOK TIME 15 minutes

Ingredients

1	T. coconut oil
6	slices of uncured bacon
30	oz. frozen shredded hash browns or sweet potato hash browns, thawed
1	green bell pepper, seeded and chopped
1	red bell pepper, seeded and chopped
1	small yellow onion, diced
	Salt and pepper, to taste
12	eggs
1	c. coconut milk
1	t. dried dill
1	t. minced garlic

Directions

SLOW

1. Grease inside of slow cooker with oil.
2. Brown bacon in skillet over medium heat. Drain on a paper towel-lined plate and crumble.
3. In a large bowl, combine potatoes, peppers, onion, salt and pepper.
4. Layer half the potato mixture, all of the bacon and then the rest of the potato mixture in the cooking vessel.
5. Combine eggs, milk, dill and garlic in a bowl; pour over the rest of the ingredients.
6. Cover and cook on LOW for 8 hours.

FAST

1. Set Crock-Pot® Express to sautè setting. Add bacon and cook until browned. Drain on a paper towel-lined plate and crumble.
2. Butter the bottom and sides of a heat-proof insert that fits inside the cooker. Combine potatoes, peppers, onion, bacon crumbles, salt and pepper in the insert.
3. In a separate bowl, combine eggs, milk, dill and garlic; pour over ingredients in the insert and cover with foil.
4. Pour 1 c. water into cooker. Add trivet and place insert on top.
5. Cover with the lid, ensuring the steam vent is closed. Cook on Poultry setting (High Pressure) for 15 minutes. Naturally release steam for 10 minutes and then serve immediately.

This casserole
could also be made
with diced ham
instead of bacon!

Bacon and Spinach Quiche

This easy-to-make meal will have your diners paying their compliments to the chef.

YIELD 8 portions **I** **SLOW COOK TIME** 4 hours **I**
EXPRESS COOK TIME 20 minutes

Ingredients

- 1 T. olive oil
- ½ c. onion, diced
- 6 eggs, whisked
- 2 T. milk
- ½ t. black pepper
- 1 c. bacon, cooked and crumbled
- 1 c. chopped fresh baby spinach, stems removed
- 1 tomato, diced
- 1 tsp. salt
- 1 c. fontina cheese, divided

Directions

SLOW

1. Grease the inside of a 4- or 5-quart slow cooker with olive oil.
2. Combine all ingredients except ¼ c. of the fontina cheese. Pour into the prepared cooker.
3. Cover and cook on LOW for 4 hours, or until a toothpick inserted in the center comes out clean.
4. Sprinkle remaining cheese on top and recover eggs. Let sit on WARM setting for 10 minutes or until cheese is melted.

FAST

1. Grease the bottom and sides of a heat-proof insert that fits inside the cooker.
2. Combine all ingredients except ¼ c. of the fontina cheese. Pour into the prepared dish. Cover with foil.
3. Pour 1 c. of water in the bottom of the cooker. Insert trivet and place prepared dish on top. Lock lid into place and ensure the steam vent is closed.
4. Cook on Beans/Chili setting (High Pressure) for 20 minutes.
5. Do a natural release of the steam for 10 minutes, then vent and carefully open lid. Test that the eggs are done to your liking. Sprinkle remaining cheese on top. Remove dish and serve immediately.

You can always swap fontina cheese for provolone, Gruyère or Gouda.

Cheesy
Hash Brown Casserole

This savory casserole will have your family and friends scrambling for seconds.

YIELD 6 portions **I** **SLOW COOK TIME** 5 hours **I**
EXPRESS COOK TIME 15 minutes

Ingredients

- 6 c. refrigerated or frozen hash browns
- ⅓ c. sliced green onions
- 1 c. frozen peas (optional)
- ½ c. cooked and crumbled bacon (optional)
- 1 t. salt
- ½ t. pepper
- 1 t. smoked paprika
- 2 c. shredded sharp cheddar cheese
- 1½ c. half-and-half

Directions

SLOW

1. Grease your slow cooker with butter. Then place hash browns, onion, peas and bacon (if using) in cooker. Sprinkle with salt, pepper and smoked paprika. Top with cheese, then pour over half-and-half.
2. Cook on LOW for 5 hours.

FAST

1. Pour 1 c. water into Crock-Pot® Express.
2. Combine all ingredients in a heatproof dish that will fit in the cooker. Cover bowl with a paper towel and foil; place in the cooker.
3. Seal lid and make sure the vent is closed. Cook on HIGH for 15 minutes, then naturally release the rest of steam.
4. Carefully remove dish and scoop or invert onto a platter.

Add Some Spice

If you're a big fan of hot sauce, this is a great recipe to add it to. But make sure to only add the hot sauce to the portion on your own plate; some of your guests might not be able to handle the casserole otherwise!

Southern Creamy Grits

This ultimate comfort food will stick to your ribs all day long.

YIELD 4 portions **I** **SLOW COOK TIME** 7 to 8 hours **I**
EXPRESS COOK TIME 10 minutes

Ingredients

- 1–2 T. butter or margarine
- 1 c. stone-ground grits (not quick cooking)
- 2 c. water
- 1½ c. milk
- ½ c. heavy cream
- 1 t. kosher salt

I love to add cheese to my grits! Just let it melt over the top.

Directions

SLOW

1. Butter the interior of a slow cooker.
2. Combine grits, water, milk, cream and salt in the cooker.
3. Cook on LOW for 7 to 8 hours or overnight.
4. Remove cooker lid and stir grits well to break up any lumps that formed during the cooking.

FAST

1. Grease the Crock-Pot® Express insert with butter and leave the remaining butter in the pot. Add remaining ingredients except the milk and cream.
2. Cover with lid and secure. Ensure steam vent is closed. Select Soup setting (High Pressure) at 10 minutes. Do a natural release of the steam for 15 minutes then quickly release any remaining steam.
3. Carefully remove lid and stir in milk and cream until desired texture is achieved. Top with cheddar cheese and serve.

Breakfast
Bread Pudding

Syrupy and sweet, this mouth-watering meal will bring you back to crisp fall days with its apple overtones and cinnamon spice.

YIELD 4 to 6 portions **I SLOW COOK TIME** 6 hours **I EXPRESS COOK TIME** 30 minutes

Ingredients

- 5   c. day-old French bread, cubed
- 3   large Granny Smith apples, peel and chopped
- 1   t. ground cinnamon
- ½   t. ground allspice
- ¼   c. brown sugar, packed
- ¼   t. salt
- 2   c. evaporated milk
- ¼   c. water
- ¼   c. pure maple syrup
- 12 oz. breakfast sausage, cooked and crumbled

Directions

SLOW

1. Grease the inside of a 4-quart slow cooker.
2. Press half of the bread cubes into the bottom of the cooker.
3. Combine the apples, cinnamon, allspice, brown sugar and salt in a mixing bowl. Add the milk, water and maple syrup to the bowl and mix well.
4. Pour half of the apple mixture over the bread in the slow cooker. Gently press down on the apples to ensure the liquid is absorbed by the bread. Spread half of the sausage over the apple mixture, followed by the remaining bread. Top the bread with the remaining sausage, followed by the remaining apple mixture. Again, gently press on the apple to ensure the liquid is absorbed by the bread.
5. Cook on LOW for 6 hours.

FAST

1. Grease a 7-inch spring form pan. Press half of the bread cubes into the bottom of the prepared pan.
2. Combine the apples, cinnamon, allspice, brown sugar and salt in a mixing bowl. Next add the milk, water and maple syrup to the bowl and mix well.
3. Pour half of the apple mixture over the bread in a spring-form pan. Gently press down on the apples to ensure the liquid is absorbed by the bread. Spread half of the sausage over the apple mixture, followed by the remaining bread. Top the bread with the remaining sausage, followed by the remaining apple mixture. Again, gently press on the apple to ensure the liquid is absorbed by the bread. Cover with foil.
4. Pour 1 c. water in the bottom of the Crock-Pot® Express and place the trivet on top. Carefully place the pan on top of the trivet. Cover and lock lid. Cook on Multigrain setting (High Pressure) for 30 minutes.
5. Release steam for 10 minutes. Then carefully remove lid. Cool for 5 minutes before serving.

This Baked Brie is just begging for some French bread!

Appetizers

With these delectable dishes, you won't leave your guests hungry as they wait for your main course to begin.

Game-Day Chicken Dip

Take the stress out of tailgate-worthy snacks with this yummy dip. Just put all the ingredients in the cooker and put your feet up! It'll do all the hard work.

YIELD 10 portions **I** **SLOW COOK TIME** 2 hours **I**
EXPRESS COOK TIME 30 minutes

Ingredients

- 2 c. cooked and shredded chicken breast
- ½ c. BBQ sauce
- ½ c. hot sauce
- 8 oz. cream cheese, softened
- ¼ c. sour cream
- 2 c. shredded cheddar cheese, divided
- 3 green onions, sliced
  Corn chips or tortilla chips, to serve

NOTE For Crock Pot® Express, start with uncooked chicken breasts (about 1½ lb.). Add ½ c. water or chicken broth.

Directions

SLOW

1. Combine chicken, sauces, cream cheese, sour cream and 1 c. cheddar cheese in a 3- to 4-quart slow cooker.
2. Smooth out dip to ensure level is even across top. Sprinkle remaining cheese and sliced green onions on top.
3. Cover and cook on LOW for 2 hours.
4. Remove lid and switch to WARM setting. Serve right from the slow cooker with corn chips or tortilla chips.

FAST

1. Add all ingredients except the cheddar cheese and sour cream to the Crock Pot® Express.
2. Cover and lock lid. Cook on the Meat/Stew setting (High Pressure) for 20 minutes.
3. When cooking is finished, let the steam naturally release for 10 minutes, then carefully open the steam valve.
4. Remove lid and take the chicken breasts out. Shred chicken and return to the pot.
5. Stir all ingredients and stir in the cheddar cheese and sour cream until dip reaches your desired consistency and taste. Serve with corn or tortilla chips.

Cheesy
Bacon-Stuffed Mushrooms

Savory and satisfying, these bite-size bits will be gone in the blink of an eye!

YIELD 10 portions **I** **SLOW COOK TIME** 1 hour 30 minutes to 2 hours **I** **EXPRESS COOK TIME** 20 minutes

Ingredients

14   oz. medium mushrooms (about 10 mushrooms)
1   c. shredded Monterey Jack cheese
¼   c. plus 2 T. breadcrumbs
1   t. garlic powder
1   egg white
6   pieces of cooked bacon
1   t. Worcestershire sauce
     Salt and pepper, to taste

NOTE For Crock Pot® Express, add 2 T. butter.

Directions

SLOW

1. Grease a large, oval slow cooker with olive oil. Using a mushroom brush, wash mushrooms under running water. Pat with paper towels to dry. Remove mushroom stems and set aside.
2. Place mushroom caps in the cooker (hollow side up) and sprinkle with salt and pepper. Mince mushroom stems and place in a medium bowl. Add shredded cheese, breadcrumbs, garlic powder, egg white, bacon pieces, Worcestershire sauce, salt and pepper with minced stems in the bowl. Mix.
3. Spoon mixture into mushroom caps and press to "stuff" mixture into mushrooms.
4. Cover and cook on HIGH for 1 hour 30 minutes to 2 hours.
5. Place on a platter to serve or serve right from the slow cooker on WARM setting.

FAST

1. Follow steps 1-4 of SLOW recipe.
2. Select the Sauté setting and melt butter in the multi-cooker. Place stuffed mushrooms in the pot and sauté for 2 minutes.
3. Remove mushrooms and place trivet in cooker. Pour in ½ c. water and place mushrooms on top of trivet. Cover with the lid and lock it into place.
4. Select Meat/Stew setting (High Pressure) and set timer to 20 minutes. Once finished, carefully do a quick release and then serve immediately.

Feel free to sub out the Monterey Jack cheese for Asiago or Fontina for an Italian twist!

Red, White & Blue
Chicken Meatballs

Show off your love for the U.S.A. with these patriotic small bites, which will have guests praising your creative twist on meatballs.

YIELD 24 portions **I SLOW COOK TIME** 4 hours **I**
EXPRESS COOK TIME 20 minutes

Ingredients

- 6 T. Italian salad dressing, divided
- ⅓ c. plus 3 T. hot sauce, divided
- 1 lb. ground chicken
- ½ c. blue cheese crumbles
-    Salt and pepper, to taste
- 1 egg
- ½ c. Italian breadcrumbs

Directions

SLOW

1. Mix 3 T. Italian dressing and ⅓ c. hot sauce together in a small bowl.
2. Combine all remaining ingredients except blue cheese in a large bowl. Pour hot sauce mixture over ingredients in large bowl. Mix well with your hands to incorporate all ingredients.
3. Make golf ball-sized meatballs with blue cheese inside. Grab a bit of meat, slightly indent with your thumb and place a few blue cheese crumbles inside. Form meatball around the cheese with firm pressure so that the cheese doesn't ooze out during cooking.
4. Continue making meatballs and place in a 6-quart slow cooker.
5. Combine remaining 3 T. Italian dressing and 3 T. hot sauce and drizzle over meatballs in the slow cooker.
6. Cover and cook on LOW for 4 hours.
7. Serve with blue cheese or ranch dressing, carrots and celery.

FAST

1. Follow steps 1-3 of the SLOW recipe.
2. Select the Sauté setting and heat 2 T. oil in cooker. Place meatballs in. the bottom of the pot. Do not overlap or crowd. Sear all side of meatballs; about 3 minutes.
3. Remove and place meatballs in an oven-proof glass bowl. Repeat steps with remaining meatballs.
4. Drizzle remaining 3 T. dressing and 3 T. hot sauce over the meatballs.
5. Pour 1 c. water in bottom of cooker. Insert trivet and place glass dish with meatballs on top.
6. Cover and lock lid. Cook on Manual/High setting for 20 minutes.
7. When cooking is finished, quick release steam. Serve immediately.

Bacon and cheese really do make everything taste better!

Cheesy Bacon Bean Dip

Bean dip doesn't need to be boring! Mix it up with this no-hassle, versatile winner.

YIELD 12 portions **I** **SLOW COOK TIME** 9 hours **I**
EXPRESS COOK TIME 1 hour

Ingredients

- 1 (14.5-oz.) can diced tomatoes
- 1 onion, chopped
  Salt and pepper, to taste
- 3 garlic cloves, minced
- 1 T. oregano
- 1 (16-oz.) package 15-Bean Soup
- 2 c. shredded cheddar cheese
- 1 package pre-cooked bacon, chopped

Directions

SLOW

1. Pour diced tomatoes (do not drain) in slow cooker. Add onion, salt, pepper, garlic and oregano.
2. Rinse and sort beans. Add to cooker. Cover ingredients in cooker with water. Water should be 1 to 2 inches above the bean line.
3. Cook on LOW overnight (or 8 hours).
4. Drain liquid and reserve.
5. Pulse bean mixture in a blender on "salsa" setting if you have it. Add reserved liquid as needed. (I had to do this in 2 batches.) If your beans are still hot, make sure to let the steam vent!
6. Return bean mixture to cooker. Add shredded cheese (I like cheddar) and bacon. Stir and cook on LOW until heated through and cheese is melted (about an hour).
7. Serve with tortilla chips or corn chips.

FAST

1. Follow steps 1-2 of the SLOW recipe using the Crock-Pot® Express.
2. Cover and seal with lid, ensuring steam vent is closed.
3. Cook for 30 minutes on Bean setting (High Pressure) followed by a 30-minute Natural Release.
4. Remove lid and follow steps 4–7 of SLOW recipe.

Tomatillo Salsa Verde

Put your go-to red salsa back on the shelf. This flavorful alternative will have you seeing green.

YIELD 8 portions **I** **SLOW COOK TIME** 3 to 4 hours **I**
EXPRESS COOK TIME 20 minutes

Appetizers

Ingredients

- 1   lb. tomatillos, husked
- ½   c. finely chopped onion
- 2   t. minced garlic
- 1   serrano chile pepper, minced
     Juice from 1–2 limes (about ¼ c. lime juice)
- ½   t. cumin
- 1   t. salt
- 1½ c. boiling water
- 2   T. chopped cilantro
- 1   T. chopped fresh oregano

NOTE Water does not need to be boiling for Crock-Pot® Express..

Directions

SLOW

1. Place tomatillos, onion, garlic and chile pepper into slow cooker. Season with lime juice, cumin and salt. Pour in boiling water.
2. Cover and cook on HIGH for 1 hour 30 minutes to 2 hours. Reduce to LOW, allowing tomatillos to become soft, for another 1 hour 30 minutes to 2 hours.
3. Stir in cilantro and oregano.
4. Using a blender or a hand blender, puree the tomatillos and water until smooth.

FAST

1. Follow step 1 of the SLOW recipe.
2. Select Steam setting at 10 minutes (High Pressure). Do a Natural Release for 10 minutes.
3. Follow steps 3-4 of SLOW recipe.

Make a Meal of It

Although this salsa makes a great stand-alone appetizer or a yummy snack, you can pair it with the Steak Fajitas (pg. 141) and the Mexican Custard Flan (pg. 220) to make a beautiful three-course dinner. Your family and friends will love it! You can even make the salsa and flan the day before.

Barbecue
Chicken Wings

These slow-cooked wings are fall-off-the-bone good and worth the wait!

YIELD 4 portions **I** **SLOW COOK TIME** 6 to 8 hours **I**
EXPRESS COOK TIME 15 minutes

Ingredients

- ⅓ c. soy sauce
- 1 t. ginger, freshly grated
- 1 t. minced garlic
- 3–4 green onions, sliced
- ¼ t. crushed red pepper flakes
- ½ c. ketchup
- ½ c. BBQ sauce
- 2 T. honey
- 2 dozen chicken wings

Directions

SLOW

1. Combine all ingredients except chicken in a 6-quart slow cooker. Stir well.
2. Place chicken wings in the sauce ingredients and mix well until they are completely covered with sauce.
3. Cover and cook on LOW for 6 to 8 hours.
4. If desired, place cooked chicken on a foil-lined baking sheet. Place under the broiler for a few minutes to brown. (This is simply to make them look as good as they taste. Do NOT leave under the broiler for too long though, or the sugar in the BBQ sauce will burn.) You can also use a grill pan if you have one handy!

FAST

1. Combine all ingredients except chicken and water to make the sauce. Reserve ½ c. of the sauce and set aside for later.
2. Trim off any excess skin and toss wings with remaining sauce.
3. Pour water into the bottom of the multi-cooker. Insert trivet and place wings on top.
4. Cover with lid and lock into place. Ensure steam vent is closed. Select Manual/High setting and set timer to 5 minutes. Cover a large baking sheet with foil and set oven to broil.
5. Once timer is finished, let the cooker naturally release steam for 10 minutes, and then carefully turn the knob to the venting position to release the rest of the steam.
6. Unlock and remove lid. Place wings on the cookie sheet, being careful not to overlap.
7. Baste with reserved sauce and broil for a few minutes, or until browned.

Serve with celery sticks and ranch or blue cheese dressing!

Hot Onion Dip

Simple and low-maintenance, this recipe will delight even the pickiest of eaters at your next get-together!

YIELD 12 to 14 portions **SLOW COOK TIME** 2 to 3 hours
EXPRESS COOK TIME 20 minutes

Ingredients

- 1 sweet onion, finely chopped
- 16 oz. cream cheese, plain
- 8 oz. chive and onion flavored cream cheese
- 2 c. Italian cheese blend, shredded
- ⅓ c. mayonnaise
- 2 garlic cloves, minced
- ½ T. Worcestershire sauce
- ½ t. seasoned salt

Directions

SLOW

1. Add butter to skillet and sauté onions over medium heat until softened. Add all packages of cream cheese to skillet and cook over low heat until softened.
2. Add cream cheese/onion mixture, Italian cheese blend, mayonnaise, garlic, Worcestershire and salt to slow cooker. Mix well.
3. Transfer from skillet; cover and cook on HIGH for 2 to 3 hours, stirring every 20 to 30 minutes.

FAST

1. Turn multi-cooker to Sauté setting.
2. Once hot, add butter and sauté onions just until they start to brown.
3. Transfer onions to an oven-safe bowl. Add remaining ingredients and mix well.
4. Pour 1 c. water in the bottom of the multi-cooker and insert trivet.
5. Place oven-safe dish on top of the trivet and secure lid into place.
6. Cook on HIGH pressure for 15 minutes and then do a natural release for 5 minutes.
7. Remove the lid and stir well. Serve immediately.

Serve with bagel chips or fresh vegetables!

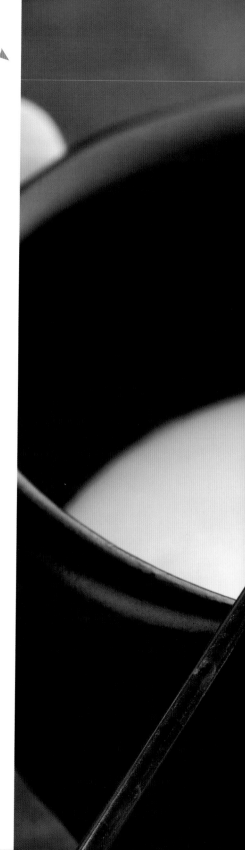

Make it your own! You can also dip vegetables, potatoes and meats in this fondue.

Havarti Cheese Fondue

Warm yourself up with this decadent fondue. It'll make the act of simply dipping bread in cheese seem luxurious.

YIELD 8 to 10 portions **I** **SLOW COOK TIME** 1 to 2 hours **I**
EXPRESS COOK TIME 10 minutes

Ingredients

- ½ c. chicken broth
- ⅓ c. milk
- 1 c. Havarti cheese, shredded
- 1½ c. shredded sharp cheddar cheese
- 1 T. all-purpose flour
- 1 (7-oz.) can artichoke hearts, drained and chopped
- ¼ c. green onions, sliced
  French bread loaf, ½-in. slices

Directions

SLOW

1. Add broth and milk to a 2-quart slow cooker.
2. Cover and cook on HIGH until simmering, about 1 hour.
3. Add cheeses, about 1 cup at a time, whisking until melted. Sprinkle in flour
4. Turn cooker to LOW, stirring cheese constantly, until cheese starts to become melted and thick. Next, add artichoke hearts and green onions; stir mixture.
5. Keep on WARM setting, and serve with sliced and toasted French bread.

FAST

1. Turn Crock-Pot® Express to Sauté setting. Add broth and milk; sauté until simmering.
2. Add cheeses, about 1 cup at a time, whisking until melted.Sprinkle in flour
3. Turn Sauté setting to LOW heat, stirring cheese constantly, until cheese starts to become melted and thick.
4. Add artichoke hearts and green onions; stir mixture. Serve immediately with sliced and toasted French bread.

Jalapeño Popper Dip

Lovers of jalapeño peppers will be clamoring for this creamy, spreadable version.

YIELD 4 to 6 portions **I SLOW COOK TIME** 1 to 2 hours **I EXPRESS COOK TIME** 25 minutes

Ingredients

- 2 (8-oz.) pkgs. cream cheese, softened
- 1 c. mayonnaise
- 1 (4-oz.) can chopped fire roasted green chilies, drained
- 1 (2-oz.) can diced jalapeño peppers, drained (If you use almost half a bottle of pre-slice jalepeños, it will tame it down a little!)
- 1 c. grated Parmesan cheese (or shredded Pizza cheese or half-and-half)

Don't use low-fat cream cheese or mayonnaise. The dip will lose its creamy texture!

Directions

SLOW

1. Combine all ingredients in the slow cooker.
2. Cover and cook on HIGH for 1 to 2 hours or until warmed through (Note: Watch for the first 20 minutes or so, stirring so that everything blends together.)
3. Turn to WARM setting once done. Serve directly from the slow cooker with tortilla chips or crackers.

FAST

1. Combine all ingredients in the Crock-Pot® Express.
2. Select Sauté setting on low heat, stirring so that everything blends together. Cover and cook for 25 minutes.
3. Switch to WARM and serve from the pot.

Mash the beans if desired for easier chip-dipping!

Chipotle
Black Bean Dip

Score a touchdown at your next game-day gathering with this crowd pleaser.

YIELD 10 to 12 portions **I** **SLOW COOK TIME** 3 to 4 hours **I**
EXPRESS COOK TIME 10 minutes

Ingredients

- 1 (8-oz.) can refried beans
- 1 (8-oz.) can kidney beans, drained and rinsed
- 1 (15-oz.) can black beans, drained and rinsed
- 1 (8-oz.) can corn
- 2 c. salsa
- 2 chipotle peppers in adobo sauce, chopped
- 2 t. adobo sauce (from can)
- 1 t. cumin
- 8 oz. shredded cheddar cheese
- 2 green onions, chopped
  Tortilla chips, for serving

Directions

SLOW

1. Set aside 1 c. of the shredded cheese and all of the green onions. Mix all remaining ingredients together in a 3.5-quart slow cooker.
2. Cover and cook on LOW for 3 to 4 hours, stirring very quickly, every hour.
3. Finish the dip by sprinkling with cheese and the green onions on top.
4. Keep cooker on WARM setting, and serve warm with tortilla chips.

FAST

1. Mix everything except the cheese and onions in the Crock-Pot® Express.
2. Cook on Beans/Chili Setting (High Pressure) for 5 minutes, with a 5-minute Natural Release.
3. Finish dip by sprinkling with cheese and green onions on top. Serve warm with tortilla chips.

You might want to make a double batch because this dip will disappear fast!

Enchilada Dip

A delicious dip that's perfect for every occasion and season.

YIELD 30 portions **I SLOW COOK TIME** 7 to 9 minutes **I EXPRESS COOK TIME** 22 minutes

Ingredients

- 2 lb. boneless, skinless chicken breasts or thighs
- 1 (10-oz.) can enchilada sauce
- 1 (10-oz.) pkg. frozen corn
- 2 (8-oz.) pkgs. cream cheese, softened
- 4 c. shredded pepper jack cheese

Directions

SLOW

1. Combine chicken and enchilada sauce in a 4-quart slow cooker.
2. Cover and cook on LOW for 6 to 8 hours or until the chicken is thoroughly cooked.
3. Shred the chicken in the sauce using two forks or shred claws and place back into the slow cooker. Put corn on top of chicken.
4. In a small bowl, stir together the softened cream cheese and pepper jack cheese. Transfer to the cooker.
5. Cover and cook for 30 minutes on LOW. Stir and cook an additional 30 minutes or until cheese is completely melted.

FAST

1. Combine chicken and enchilada sauce in Crock-Pot® Express. Cover and lock lid. Make sure steam vent is sealed.
2. Cook on Manual/High setting for 6 minutes. Let the steam release naturally for 5 minutes and then turn valve for quick release.
3. Remove chicken and place aside to rest. Add remaining ingredients to the cooker and stir. Shred or chop the chicken and add back to the cooker.
4. Cook on Manual/High setting for 6 minutes. Let the steam release naturally for 5 minutes and then turn valve for quick release.
5. Stir and serve immediately.

Asian-Style Pork Ribs

Turn this dish into an entree by serving over a bed of rice or greens!

This scrumptious appetizer is even better than take-out!

YIELD 6 portions **I** **SLOW COOK TIME** 3 to 5 hours **I**
EXPRESS COOK TIME 40 minutes

Ingredients

2–3 lb. pork ribs
1   c. apple cider vinegar
1   c. white vinegar
1½ c. chicken broth
1   t. sea salt, plus more to taste
1   t. black pepper
1   t. garlic powder
2   T. rice wine vinegar
2   T. sake (rice wine)
2   T. soy sauce
    Sesame seeds, for garnish
    Sliced scallions, for garnish
3   T. honey (optional)
¼   water, plus 2 T. cornstarch
    (optional)

Directions

SLOW

1. Place ribs in slow cooker and cover with apple cider vinegar, white vinegar and chicken broth. Add sea salt and let ribs sit overnight refrigerated.
2. Drain the ribs in morning. Rub both sides gently with generous amounts of sea salt, black pepper and garlic powder.
3. Place ribs upright in the cooker. Add the rice wine vinegar, sake and soy sauce.
4. Cover and cook on HIGH for 3 to 5 hours. Garnish with sesame seeds and scallions, if desired.

FAST

1. Follow steps 1-2 of SLOW recipe.
2. Add the rice wine vinegar, Saki and soy sauce to the bottom of the Crock Pot® Express. Place a trivet in cooker and place ribs upright on trivet, out of liquid.
3. Cover and lock lid, ensuring that the steam vent is closed. Cook on the Meat/Stew setting for 20 minutes. Do a Natural Release for 20 minutes.
4. If desired, set ribs aside and carefully remove trivet. Switch cooker to Sauté setting. Whisk in honey followed by water-cornstarch mixture. Bring to a simmer and continue cooking until sauce thickens. Baste ribs with sauce before serving.
5. Garnish with sesame seeds and scallions, if desired.

Roasted Garlic White Bean Dip

Impress your guests with your cooking prowess by making this elegant dip.

YIELD 15 portions | **SLOW COOK TIME** 2 hours | **EXPRESS COOK TIME** 10 minutes

Ingredients

- ¼ c. plus 1 T. extra-virgin olive oil
- 6 garlic cloves, minced
- 2 (15½-oz.) cans cannellini beans
- ⅓ c. water
- 1 c. whole milk ricotta cheese
- ¾ c. freshly grated Parmesan cheese
- 2 t. freshly chopped rosemary
- ½ t. salt
- ¼ t. black pepper
  Juice of ½ lemon
- 1 t. lemon zest
  Dash of hot sauce

Directions

SLOW

1. Heat 1 T. oil in skillet over medium-low. Add garlic and cook for a few minutes, until it becomes fragrant but not browned.
2. Place drained beans and water in a blender. Add garlic from skillet, ricotta, Parmesan, rosemary, salt, pepper and lemon juice. Blend on medium speed.
3. While blender is still on medium speed, slowly drizzle in remaining ¼ c. olive oil.
4. Place bean mixture in a small slow cooker.
5. Cover and cook on LOW for 2 hours or until heated through.
6. Stir in lemon zest, then taste and adjust seasonings before serving.

FAST

1. Heat oil in Crock-Pot® Express on Sauté setting. Add garlic and cook a few minutes until it becomes fragrant but not brown/burnt.
2. Follow steps 2-3 of SLOW recipe.
3. Place bean mixture in cooker. Sauté on low heat until heated through, about 10 minutes.
4. Stir in lemon zest, then taste and adjust seasonings before serving.

Add some Kalamata olives for some extra flavor!

Balsamic Baked Brie

Buttery, creamy and melted Brie makes for an amazing France-inspired appetizer.

YIELD 6 portions **I** **SLOW COOK TIME** 1 hour 30 minutes **I**
EXPRESS COOK TIME 30 minutes

Ingredients

- 8 oz. wheel of Brie cheese
- ⅓ c. dried fruit, chopped
- 1 T. brown sugar
- 1 T. water
- ½ t. balsamic vinegar
- ¼ c. toasted almond slivers

Directions

SLOW

1. Remove Brie from the wrapper and place in a small slow cooker.
2. Combine all other ingredients except nuts in a small bowl and place on top of the Brie.
3. Cover and cook on HIGH for 1 hour.
4. Sprinkle nuts on top of cheese. Cover and cook for 30 more minutes on HIGH.

FAST

1. Follow steps 1-2 of SLOW recipe with Crock-Pot® Express.
2. Cook on the Sauté setting on LOW heat for 30 minutes or until heated through.
3. Stir in lemon zest, then taste and adjust seasonings before serving.

Top It Off

The best part about Baked Brie is that you can add nearly whatever you'd like to it—from dried fruits to nuts—to add more flavor! If you don't want to deviate from my recipe, you could also put jars of jam alongside your Brie and crackers spread. Brie goes well with most jam varieties!

Break into this bowl of Cheesy Cauliflower!

Sides

Supplement your meal with these tasty sides. They're so good you might be tempted to make them the main course.

Creamed
Spinach

Rich and velvety, this dish will help you get your greens in for the day without it seeming like a chore.

YIELD 4 portions **I SLOW COOK TIME** 4 hours **I**
EXPRESS COOK TIME 10 minutes

Ingredients

- ⅛   c. minced onions
- 1   c. milk
- ½   c. cream cheese
- ¼   c. shredded mozzarella cheese
- ¼   c. shredded Parmesan cheese
- 2   T. butter
- ½   t. nutmeg
- 12   oz. fresh baby spinach

Directions

SLOW

1. Combine onion, milk, cheeses, butter and nutmeg and put into the slow cooker.

Serve this side with the Balsamic Pork Tenderloin on pg. 209.

2. Cover and cook on LOW for 2 hours, stirring every 30 minutes or until ingredients are melted.
3. Add baby spinach, but don't stir yet!
4. Cover again and set slow cooker to HIGH for 30 minutes. Stir well and serve immediately.

FAST

1. Turn the Crock-Pot® Express to the Sauté setting (HIGH). Add butter to pot and melt it. Add minced onions and sauté for 1 minute.
2. Add spinach, stir a few times and set lid on top until wilted, about 3 minutes.
3. Stir in remaining ingredients and continue stirring until cheese are melted.
4. Season to taste with salt before serving.

Bacon White Cheddar Au Gratin Potatoes

This perfect combo of bacon, cheese and potatoes will complement any main dish.

YIELD 6 to 8 portions I **SLOW COOK TIME** 5 hours I
EXPRESS COOK TIME TK

Ingredients

- 6 large russet potatoes, peeled and thinly sliced
- ½ lb. bacon, cooked and crumbled
- 1 t. salt
- ½ t. white pepper
- 2 c. half-and-half
- 4 T. flour
- 2 c. freshly grated white cheddar cheese

NOTE Add 1½ c. water for Crock-Pot® Express.

Directions

SLOW

1. Grease a 6-quart slow cooker with butter. Layer potatoes and bacon in slow cooker, adding salt and pepper in between layers.
2. Add half-and-half to a small saucepan and heat on medium. Once warm, whisk in flour until there are no lumps.
3. Add white cheddar cheese and whisk for a minute or two, until all the cheese is melted.
4. Remove pan from heat and pour cheese mixture over the potatoes in the cooker. Gently lift potato layers to ensure sauce is dispersed evenly.
5. Cover and cook on LOW for 5 hours or until potatoes are cooked to your desired doneness.

FAST

1. Add potato slices and 1 c. water to the Crock-Pot® Express. Cover and cook on High Pressure for 1 minute. Do a quick release of the steam. Drain water and remove potatoes from the pot.
2. Change the cooker setting to Sauté (High) and add the half-and-half. Once warm, whisk in flour until there are no lumps.
3. Add white cheddar cheese and whisk for a minute or two, until all the cheese is melted.
4. Meanwhile, layer the potatoes with bacon in an ovenproof dish that fits in cooker (about 7 in.), adding salt and pepper in between layers.
5. Pour cheese mixture over potatoes. Gently lift layers to ensure sauce is dispersed evenly.
6. Cover tightly with foil. Put a trivet in cooker and pour in ½ c. water. Place baking dish on top of trivet and cook on High Pressure for 5 minutes followed by a natural release.

Transfer it to a baking dish and place it under a broiler to brown the top!

Authentic
German Potato Salad

This picnic-basket staple is a welcome sight at any family or community gathering.

YIELD 6 portions | **SLOW COOK TIME** 6 hours |
EXPRESS COOK TIME 6 minutes

Sides

Ingredients

- 2 lb. red potatoes, cut into ¼-in. slices
- 1 small red onion, thinly sliced
- ⅓ c. apple cider vinegar
- 3 T. olive oil
- 2 tsp. Dijon mustard
- 1 T. sugar
    Salt and pepper, to taste
- 3 T. sliced green onion, for garnish
- 3 T. cooked bacon pieces, for garnish

NOTE Add 1 c. water for Crock-Pot® Express.

Directions

SLOW

1. Layer the onions and potatoes in the bottom of a 6-quart slow cooker.
2. In a small bowl, combine vinegar, oil, mustard and sugar.
3. Pour mustard mixture over top ingredients in the cooker. Toss well to coat. Then add salt and pepper.
4. Cover and cook on LOW for 6 hours. Remove lid and taste potatoes. Adjust seasoning.
5. If desired, garnish with green onion and bacon. Serve warm.

FAST

1. Pour water in the bottom of the Crock-Pot® Express. Add steam basket.
2. Layer the onions and potatoes in the steam basket. Cover with lid and make sure the steam vent is closed.
3. Cook for 6 minutes on the Rice setting (High Pressure). Do a quick release of the pressure.
4. In a small bowl, combine dressing ingredients: vinegar, oil, mustard and sugar.
5. Pour dressing over top of the potatoes and toss well to coat. Add salt and pepper.
6. If desired, garnish with green onion and bacon. Serve warm.

I grew up on German Potato Salad, and this is my favorite recipe!

Broccoli Cheese Casserole

Instead of standing over the stove for an hour, just toss this in the slow cooker and it'll be done by dinnertime!

YIELD 8 portions **|** **SLOW COOK TIME** 4 hours 15 minutes to 5 hours 15 minutes **|** **EXPRESS COOK TIME** 10 minutes

Ingredients

- 1 (10¾-oz.) can condensed cream of mushroom soup
- 1 c. mayonnaise
- 1 egg, beaten
- 1 t. garlic powder
  Salt and pepper, to taste
- ½ yellow onion, finely chopped
- 30 oz. frozen chopped broccoli
- 10 oz. shredded sharp cheddar cheese, divided
- 2 pinches paprika

NOTE Add 1 c. water for Crock-Pot® Express.

Directions

SLOW

1. Lightly grease the insert of a 4-quart slow cooker.
2. Mix together soup, mayonnaise, egg, garlic powder, salt, pepper and onion in a medium bowl.
3. Break up the frozen broccoli in a separate bowl.
4. Spoon the soup and mayonnaise mixture over the broccoli, and mix well. Add in 8 oz. of cheese and mix well.
5. Transfer mixture to the prepared cooker and spread evenly.
6. Cover and cook on LOW for 5 hours or on HIGH for 4 hours.
7. Sprinkle with remaining cheese and paprika. Cover and cook 15 more minutes, or until cheese melts.

FAST

1. Lightly grease an ovenproof dish that fits in the Crock-Pot® Express.
2. Mix together condensed soup, mayonnaise, egg, garlic powder, salt, pepper and onion in a medium bowl.
3. Break up the frozen broccoli in a separate bowl. Spoon the soup and mayonnaise mixture over the broccoli and mix well.
4. Add in 8 oz. of shredded cheese and stir until well combined.
5. Transfer mixture to the prepared dish and spread evenly. Cover dish with foil. Pour water into cooker and add trivet. Place dish with broccoli on the trivet.
6. Close lid, lock and close steam vent. Cook on Steam setting (High Pressure) for 10 minutes. Quick release steam.
7. Carefully pull back foil and sprinkle broccoli with remaining cheese and paprika. Recover dish and allow for cheese to melt before serving.

Don't forget to thoroughly mix the ingredients together.

Spanish Rice

Switch out your bland sides for this flavorful recipe. It'll spice up your dinner table!

YIELD 6 to 8 portions | **SLOW COOK TIME** 2 hours 30 minutes to 3 hours 30 minutes | **EXPRESS COOK TIME** 13 minutes

Ingredients

- 2 T. olive oil (optional)
- 1 medium onion (optional)
- 1 green bell pepper (optional)
- 2 c. basmati rice, or long or short grain brown rice, uncooked
- 2 c. chicken broth, vegetable broth or water
- 1 (14.5-oz.) can diced tomatoes
  Optional veggies: carrot, zucchini, etc. (finely chopped)
- 2 t. chili powder
- 2 t. cumin
- 1 t. sea salt
- 2 T. chopped fresh cilantro, for garnish

Directions

SLOW

1. If desired, heat oil and sauté onion and pepper in a skillet, adding the rice for additional flavor.
2. Grease the slow cooker, and transfer the rice, pepper and onion.
3. Add the remainder of the ingredients except the cilantro, and stir to combine, adding in any additional veggies you will enjoy.
4. Cover and cook on HIGH for 2 hours 30 minutes to 3 hours 30 minutes.

FAST

1. Set Crock-Pot® Express to Sauté setting and heat oil. Add onion and pepper and cook for a few minutes to soften.
2. Add the remainder of the ingredients except the cilantro. Cover and lock lid into place. Ensure steam vent is closed.
3. Cook on Rice setting (High Pressure) for 3 minutes. Naturally Release pressure for 10 minutes.
4. Remove lid and fluff rice. Garnish with cilantro. Serve immediately.

After the rice has absorbed the chicken broth, it's done!

Sides

Green Bean Casserole

This low-maintenance casserole can be tossed in the slow cooker so you can take care of you!

YIELD 6 to 8 portions | **SLOW COOK TIME** 5 to 6 hours |
EXPRESS COOK TIME 15 minutes

Ingredients

- 2 (10-oz.) bags frozen green beans
- 1 (14.8-oz.) can cream of mushroom soup
- ⅓ c. milk
- ¼ t. salt
- ¼ t. black pepper
- 1 (2.8-oz.) can French-fried onions

Directions

SLOW

1. Mix together the green beans, soup and milk in a slow cooker.
2. Sprinkle with salt and pepper and half of the French-fried onions.
3. Cover and cook on LOW for 5 to 6 hours. Top with remaining onions just before serving.

FAST

1. Mix together green beans, soup and milk in an ovenproof dish that fits in the Crock-Pot® Express.
2. Sprinkle with salt and pepper and half of the French-fried onions. Cover with foil.
3. Lock lid into place and close steam vent. Cook on Soup setting (High Pressure) for 5 minutes followed by 10 minutes natural release. Top with remaining onions just before serving.

Spice It Up

Green Bean Casserole has been a family Thanksgiving staple since it was created by Campbell's in 1955. If you want to add a twist to this classic, add a dash of garlic powder or smoked paprika. It will add just enough flavor so a family member asks, "Wow! What's your secret?"

Asparagus and Fennel Risotto

Impress your guests with this delectable dish that will have them begging for your recipe.

YIELD 8 portions **I** **SLOW COOK TIME** 2 to 3 hours **I**
EXPRESS COOK TIME 20 minutes

Ingredients

1	t. ground fennel
1	fennel bulb, finely chopped
1	c. arborio rice, uncooked
1	bunch asparagus spears, chopped
1	c. sliced mushrooms (optional)
2	T. finely chopped shallots
2	t. minced garlic
2	c. chicken stock
1	c. water, divided
⅓	c. white wine
½	c. Parmesan cheese
1	T. lemon zest
	Salt and pepper, to taste

NOTE Add 2 T. butter to FAST ingredients.

Directions

SLOW

1. Grease slow cooker with olive oil. Combine ground fennel, rice, asparagus, mushrooms (if using), shallots and garlic; add to cooker.
2. Add chicken broth, water and wine to rice mixture; stir to combine.
3. Cover and cook on LOW for 2 to 3 hours, or until the rice is tender but remains a bit sticky and creamy.
4. Stir Parmesan, lemon zest, salt and pepper into the risotto.
5. Add a little extra hot water to risotto if you desire a creamier dish.

FAST

1. Use Sauté function and melt butter in the Crock-Pot® Express. Add shallots and fennel. Sauté just until softened, then add garlic. Sauté 1 more minute.
2. Pour in chicken broth, water and wine. Stir in remaining ingredients.
3. Cover and lock lid, ensuring the steam vent is closed. Cook on Rice/Risotto setting (High Pressure) for 10 minutes. Do a Natural Release for 10 minutes and then carefully turn vent to release remaining steam.
4. Gently stir, then serve.

Feel free to shave some extra Parmesan over your finished product!

Sides

Mexican
Quinoa and Beans

Packed with protein, this healthier spin on traditional rice and beans will have you feeling full and satisfied.

YIELD 6 portions | **SLOW COOK TIME** 2 hours |
EXPRESS COOK TIME 24 minutes

Ingredients

- 1 (14-oz.) can black beans, drained and rinsed
- 1 c. quinoa, rinsed
- 2 c. chicken broth, vegetable broth or coconut water
- ¾ c. salsa verde
- ¼ c. corn, whole kernel
- 1 t. cumin
- 1 t. sea salt
- 2 garlic cloves, minced
  Salt and pepper, to taste
  Lime juice

Directions

SLOW

1. Add beans, quinoa, broth, salsa, corn, cumin, sea salt and garlic to slow cooker.
2. Cover and cook on HIGH for 2 hours.
3. Fluff quinoa with a fork.

4. Add fresh lime juice to your liking; sprinkle with sea salt and pepper to taste.

FAST

1. Add all ingredients to the Crock-Pot® Express.
2. Cover and lock lid; close steam vent. Cook on Rice/Risotto setting (Low Pressure) for 12 minutes. Turn cooker off and let pressure naturally release for 12 minutes.
3. Turn steam vent to release remaining steam and carefully remove lid.
4. Stir gently, then serve immediately with a few lime slices.

Add cooked chicken, tomatoes and avocado to make this side a full meal. ⋯⋯➤

Guinness Baked Beans

Bring these beans to your next BBQ. They'll complement anything that's on the grill.

YIELD 16 to 20 portions **| SLOW COOK TIME** 5 to 6 hours **|**
EXPRESS COOK TIME 10 minutes

Ingredients

- 6   slices of bacon
- 1   onion, minced
- 2   (20-oz.) cans red kidney beans, drained and rinsed
- 2   (20-oz.) cans cannellini beans, drained and rinsed
- 1   c. ketchup
- 2   T. Worcestershire sauce
- 4   T. tomato paste
- 12 oz. Guinness, or similar beer
- ¼   c. brown sugar
- 1   t. dry mustard
- 1   t. smoked paprika
- 2   T. honey
- Salt and pepper, to taste
- 1   t. hot sauce (optional)

Directions

SLOW

1. Cook bacon in a heavy skillet. Sed aside on paper towels to drain, leaving in grease.
2. Add onions to the skillet with bacon grease and cook over low heat to sweat onions until transluscent.
3. Using a slotted spoon, remove onions from grease and place in a 5-quart slow cooker.
4. Top with the drained and rinsed beans, ketchup, Worcestershire, tomato paste, Guinness, brown sugar, mustard, smoked paprika, honey, crumbled bacon, salt, pepper and hot sauce (if using).
5. Cover and cook on LOW for 5 to 6 hours.

FAST

1. Set Crock-Pot® Express to Sauté (High). Add bacon and cook until browned. Set aside bacon on paper towels to drain then crumble once cooled.
2. Reduce heat to LOW and add onions to the cooker. Sauté until almost translucent, then turn cooker off.
3. Drain onions on a paper towel and carefully use a paper towel to wipe grease from pot. (Do not clean.)
4. Add all ingredients to the cooker: onions, drained and rinsed beans, ketchup, Worcestershire, tomato paste, Guinness, brown sugar, mustard, smoked paprika, honey, crumbled bacon, salt and pepper. Add hot sauce, if desired.
5. Cover and lock lid; close steam vent. Cook on Beans/Chili setting for 5 minutes followed by 5 minutes Natural Release.
6. Stir before serving.

Sides

Butternut Squash Casserole

Fluffy and creamy with a little crunch, this will melt in your mouth.

YIELD 6 portions **| SLOW COOK TIME** 1 hour 45 minutes to 7 hours 30 minutes **| EXPRESS COOK TIME** 1 hour 20 minutes

Ingredients

- 2 medium butternut squash, peeled and cut into chunks
- ½ c. sugar
- 2 eggs
- ¼ c. milk
- 2 T. butter
- 1 t. vanilla extract
- ¼ t. ground cinnamon
- ¼ t. ground nutmeg

TOPPING

- ½ c. puffed rice cereal
- ¼ c. brown sugar
- ¼ c. chopped pecans
- 2 T. melted butter

NOTE Add 2 c. water for Crock-Pot® Express.

Directions

SLOW

1. Cover squash with water in a large saucepan; bring to a boil.
2. Reduce heat. Keep covered and simmer for 10 to 12 minutes or until tender. Drain.
3. Place squash in a medium bowl. Using an immersion blender, beat squash until smooth. Mix remaining ingredients and beat well into the squash.
4. Spray insert with cooking spray and transfer mixture to cooker.
5. Cover and cook on LOW for 5 hours 30 minutes to 7 hours 30 minutes or on HIGH for 1 hour 45 minutes to 2 hours 45 minutes.
6. Optional: Mix rice cereal, brown sugar, pecans and butter together and sprinkle over casserole during the last 30 to 45 minutes.

FAST

1. Put trivet in Crock-Pot® Express and pour in 1 c. water. Place entire squash in the cooker and cover/lock lid.
2. Close steam vent and cook on Soup setting (High Pressure) for 5 minutes. Naturally Release pressure for 1 hour.
3. Remove lid and allow squash to cool on a cutting board. Carefully cut squash length-wise and scoop out seeds. Scoop out flesh and place in bowl. Beat until smooth.
4. Blend in remaining ingredients.
5. Butter an ovenproof insert and transfer ingredients from mixing bowl. Cover with foil.
6. Pour 1 c. water in the bottom of the cooker. Set dish on top of trivet and close and lock the lid.
7. Close steam vent and cook on Beans/Chili setting for 5 minutes with 10 minutes Natural Release.

Test the center of the casserole to make sure it reads 160 degrees F before serving.

Place in an oven-safe dish, top with shredded cheese and place under the broiler to brown the top.

Cheesy Cauliflower

Even your younger guests who think veggies are "gross," will love this side!

YIELD 12 portions | **SLOW COOK TIME** 4 to 7 hours | **EXPRESS COOK TIME** 10 minutes

Ingredients

- 2 heads of cauliflower, cut into florets
- 1 onion, diced
- 1 fennel bulb, top removed, sliced
  Salt and pepper, to taste
- ½ t. paprika
- 1 jar cheddar cheese pasta sauce
- TK ham, diced (optional)

NOTE Add 1 c. water for Crock-Pot® Express.

Directions

SLOW

1. Add cauliflower, onions and fennel to a large bowl.
2. Sprinkle with salt, pepper and paprika (smoked paprika is great, too!).
3. Pour pasta sauce over ingredients in the bowl and toss to coat well.
4. Grease a slow cooker with salted butter and transfer ingredients from bowl to the cooker.
5. Cover and cook on LOW for 6 to 7 hours or on HIGH for 4 hours or until cauliflower is softened.

FAST

1. Add cauliflower, onions and fennel to an oven safe dish. Sprinkle with salt, pepper and paprika.
2. Pour pasta sauce over ingredients in the bowl and toss to coat well. Cover with foil.
3. Pour 1 c. water into the Crock-Pot® Express and insert trivet. Place dish on the trivet.
4. Lock lid into place and make sure steam vent is closed.
5. Cook on Beans setting for 5 minutes then naturally release for 5 minutes.
6. Stir cauliflower and season with salt and pepper before serving.

Balsamic
Brussels Sprouts

The tasty balsamic vinegar brings out the best flavors in this occasionally maligned vegetable.

YIELD 4 to 6 portions **|** **SLOW COOK TIME** 2 hours **|**
EXPRESS COOK TIME 7 minutes

Ingredients

- 1 lb. fresh Brussels sprouts, trimmed and halved
- ¼ c. balsamic vinegar
- 1 T. pure maple syrup
- ½ c. water
- 4 sprigs fresh thyme
  Salt and pepper, to taste
  Crumbled bacon (optional)

NOTE Add 2 T. olive oil to Fast ingredients.

Directions

SLOW

1. Trim and halve the Brussels sprouts and place in a 3-quart slow cooker. Sprinkle with salt and pepper.
2. In a small saucepan, heat the vinegar and maple syrup until boiling. Reduce heat and stir in water. Pour over sprouts in the cooker and stir.
3. Cook on HIGH for 2 hours, adding the thyme sprigs when there are just 30 minutes left to cook.
4. Before serving, discard the thyme sprigs.

FAST

1. Use the Sauté setting and heat olive oil. Sauté trimmed Brussels sprouts for 3 minutes or just until browned.
2. Add vinegar, maple syrup and water. Sauté 1 more minute.
3. Sprinkle with salt and pepper, add sprigs of thyme and bacon crumbles.
4. Cover and lock lid into place; close steam vent. Cook on Beans setting (High Pressure) for 2 minutes then Natural Release for 5 minutes.
5. Carefully remove lid, discard thyme and stir ingredients. Season to taste and serve.

Crumble bacon and sprinkle it over the sprouts before serving!

Buttery
Garlic Mushrooms

This classy side is the perfect accompaniment to the Braised Leg of Lamb (pg. 194).

YIELD 6 portions **I** **SLOW COOK TIME** 3 hours **I**
EXPRESS COOK TIME 15 minutes

Ingredients

- 2 T. olive oil
- 4 T. unsalted butter, divided
- 1 lb. baby bella, or small mushroom of your choice
- 1 T. minced garlic
- ¼ c. white wine
- ¼ c. chicken broth
- 1 T. herbs de provence
- 1 T. chopped fresh parsley, for garnish
-    Salt and pepper, to taste

Directions

SLOW

1. Place all ingredients except parsley and 1 T. butter in the slow cooker and stir.

2. Cover and cook on LOW for 3 hours.
3. Carefully remove lid and stir mushrooms. Add the last tablespoon of butter plus salt and pepper, to taste.
4. Garnish with fresh parsley when serving.

FAST

1. Turn Crock-Pot® Express on Sauté setting and add oil. Once hot, add mushrooms and brown for about 5 minutes.
2. Add remaining ingredients except parsley and 1 T. butter
3. Cover with lid and lock into place. Ensure steam vent is closed. Cook on Bean setting for 10 minutes. Use natural release for 5 minutes.
4. Carefully remove lid and stir mushrooms. Add the last tablespoon of butter plus salt and pepper, to taste.
5. Garnish with fresh parsley when serving.

It's deicious on its own or spooned over warm bread!

Loaded
Twice Baked Potatoes

Cheesy and rich, these potatoes are so good we baked them twice!

YIELD 8 portions | **SLOW COOK TIME** 8 hours 25 minutes | **EXPRESS COOK TIME** 25 minutes

Ingredients

- 8 potatoes, baking, small (about 6 oz. each)
- ⅛ t. plus ¼ t. kosher salt, divided
- ¼ c. fat-free milk
- ¼ c. plain Greek yogurt
- 2 oz. shredded sharp cheddar cheese, divided
- ¼ t. kosher salt
- ¼ t. black pepper, freshly ground
- 1 T. chopped, fresh chives
- 2 bacon slices, cooked and crumbled

NOTE Add ¾ c. water for Crock-Pot® Express.

Directions

SLOW

1. Wash potatoes, rinse and pat dry with paper towels. Spray potatoes with cooking spray and pierce with a fork. Rub ⅛ t. kosher salt evenly over potatoes.
2. Place seasoned potatoes in an oval 6-quart slow cooker. Cover and cook on LOW for 8 hours or until potatoes are tender.
3. Cool slightly, then cut each potato in half lengthwise; scoop out insides into a microwave-safe bowl, leaving an ⅛-inch-thick shell.
4. With a potato masher, mash insides. Stir in milk, yogurt, ¼ c. cheese, ¼ t. kosher salt and pepper.
5. Place in a microwave on HIGH for 1 minute or until thoroughly heated.
6. Spoon potato mixture evenly into shells, sprinkle with the remaining ¼ c. cheese.
7. Place potato halves in bottom of cooker. Cover again and cook on HIGH for approximately 25 minutes or until thoroughly heated and cheese melts.
8. Sprinkle each potato half with about ½ t. chives and about 1 t. bacon.

FAST

1. Wash potatoes and prick each one about 10 times with a fork.
2. Pour water in the bottom of the Crock-Pot® Express. Insert trivet and place prepped potatoes on top in a single layer (make sure they are not touching the water).
3. Cover with lid and lock into place. Close steam vent. Cook on Beans/Chili (High Pressure) setting for 12 minutes; Naturally Release steam for 10 minutes.
4. Cut each potato in half lengthwise; scoop out pulp into a bowl, leaving an ⅛-inch-thick shell.
5. Mash potato pulp and add in milk, yogurt, cheese, salt and pepper.
6. Spoon potato mixture evenly into shells and sprinkle with cheese, chives and bacon.
7. Place potato halves in an ovenproof dish and cover with foil. Place dish on the trivet in the cooker.
8. Cook on the Beans/Chili setting for 3 minutes followed by a quick release. Carefully remove lid and foil; serve immediately.

You don't have to use bacon—add chopped broccoli, garlic or hot sauce to switch it up!

Yummy
Mac and Cheese

It's not a classic American dinner without this beloved pasta side on the table.

YIELD 20 portions **I** **SLOW COOK TIME** 5 hours **I** **EXPRESS COOK TIME** 5 minutes

Ingredients

20	oz. elbow macaroni
1	t. minced garlic
1	medium white onion, minced
2	eggs
1	t. salt
¾	t. white pepper
12	oz. evaporated milk
1¼	c. milk
1	t. ground mustard
¾	c. salted butter, melted
32	oz. Velveeta cheese, cubed
8	oz. plus 2 c. shredded cheddar cheese, divided
6	slices bacon, cooked and crumbled (optional)

NOTE Do not use eggs or milk for Crock-Pot® Express. Decrease Velveeta to 16 oz. Do not use regular milk.

Directions

SLOW

1. Cook noodles according to package directions and transfer to a buttered 6-quart slow cooker.
2. Stir in minced garlic and onion.
3. In a small bowl, gently whisk eggs with salt and pepper.
4. Combine evaporated milk, milk, ground and melted butter and stir into whisked egg.
5. Gently stir in the cubed Velveeta and cheddar cheese with the noodles, making sure some of the cheese remains on the top.
6. Pour egg mixture over the noodles and cheese and slightly press down to allow it to seep through the layers of ingredients. Do not stir.
7. Sprinkle remaining shredded cheese and bacon pieces over top ingredients. Do not stir.
8. Cover and cook on LOW for 5 hours. Stir well and serve with more bacon crumbles on top.

FAST

1. Add noodles, 4 c. water, butter, mustard, garlic, onion, salt and pepper to the Crock-Pot Express®.
2. Cover and lock lid, ensuring steam vent is closed. Select Soup setting (High Pressure) and set time at 5 minutes. Use a hot pad and carefully open steam vent for a quick pressure release.
3. Remove lid and stir pasta to break up clumps. Stir in evaporated milk, cheddar and Velveeta until melted and combined. Top with bacon before serving.

Sides

Perfect
Corn on the Cob

Say hello to juicy, crunchy corn with this easy recipe—no grill needed!

YIELD 8 portions **|** **SLOW COOK TIME** 2 hours **|**
EXPRESS COOK TIME 2 minutes

Ingredients

8   ears of corn, shucked and
    cleaned
    Aluminum foil
    Butter, salt and pepper,
    for serving

NOTE Foil is not necessary for the Fast version, but you may have to cook in batches so the ears of corn do not overlap.

Directions

SLOW

1. Wrap each ear of corn in aluminum foil.
2. Place the foil-wrapped corn in the slow cooker. Do not add water.
3. Cover and cook on HIGH for 2 hours.
4. Serve with butter, salt and pepper.

FAST

1. Cut corn cobs in half.
2. Pour 2 c. water into the Crock-Pot® Express. Add steam basket and place corn inside; make sure not to overlap.
3. Cover and lock lid; close steam vent. Cook on Soup setting (High Pressure) but press Cancel after 2 minutes.
4. Quick release steam and carefully remove lid.
5. Remove corn and serve immediately.

Cut your corn in half for easy eating!

Mushroom Wild Rice

Your guests will go wild for this low-maintenance side dish.

YIELD 14 portions **I SLOW COOK TIME** 7 to 8 hours **I**
EXPRESS COOK TIME 42 minutes

Ingredients

- 2¼ c. water
- 10½ oz. condensed beef consomme, undiluted (or vegetable for vegetarians)
- 10½ oz. condensed French onion soup, undiluted
- 1 (12-oz.) can mushrooms, drained (or fresh mushrooms)
- 1 carrot, sliced thin (optional)
- ½ c. butter, melted
- 1 c. brown rice, uncooked (or rice of your choice)
- 1 c. wild rice, uncooked (or rice of your choice)

Directions

SLOW
1. Combine all ingredients in a 5-quart slow cooker.
2. Cover and cook on LOW for 7 to 8 hours or until rice is tender.

FAST
1. Heat Crock-Pot® Express on Sauté setting; add butter.
2. Once butter is melted, add mushroom pieces, salt and pepper. Sauté 3 minutes. Add remaining ingredients, stir.
3. Cover with lid and lock into place. Be sure that steam vent is closed. Cook 30 minutes on High Pressure followed by 12 minutes natural release.
4. Fluff with fork and serve.

Make a Meal

Lots of sides just need a bit of extra protein to turn into a complete meal! Add leftover chicken, turkey or even a couple cans of black beans to this dish to make a quick, easy meal that's perfect to pack for lunches.

Sides

I like mine with extra butter and honey!

Country
Cornbread

Cornbread that's just like what your grandma used to make.

YIELD 6 portions | **SLOW COOK TIME** 1 hour 30 minutes to 3 hours | **EXPRESS COOK TIME** 20 minutes

Ingredients

1¼ c. flour
¾   c. yellow cornmeal
¼   c. sugar
4½ t. baking powder
1   t. salt
1   egg, lightly beaten
1   c. milk
⅓   c. melted butter

Directions

SLOW

1. Mix the flour, cornmeal, sugar, baking powder and salt in a bowl.
2. Add the egg, milk and melted butter. Stir until just moistened.
3. Place batter in a greased loaf pan that will fit in your large slow cooker. Place pan in the cooker then pour ¾ c. of water around the pan. Alternatively: Line the cooker with foil and grease generously, then pour batter directly in the cooker.
4. Cover and cook for 1 hour 30 minutes to 3 hours on HIGH.

FAST

1. Follow steps 1–2 of the SLOW recipe. Place batter in a greased loaf pan.
2. Pour 1 c. water in the Crock-Pot® Express and insert trivet.
3. Tightly cover pan with foil and place it on the trivet
4. Cover with lid, lock and close the steam vent. Cook on Multigrain setting (High Pressure) for 20 minutes followed by a quick release.
5. Carefully uncover and remove bread from the cooker. Allow to cool for 5 minutes before slicing.

Soups

There's nothing a hot bowl of slow-cooked soup can't fix. With the variety of soups in this section, you could have a different soup every day for weeks!

Tortellini
and soup is
a winning
combination!

Cajun 15 Bean Stew

This flavorful stew will warm you up on the coldest of nights.

YIELD 8 to 10 portions | **SLOW COOK TIME** 8 hours |
EXPRESS COOK TIME 1 hour

Ingredients

- 2 carrots, peeled and sliced
- ½ large white onion, sliced
- 3 pieces of bacon, cooked and crumbled
- 2 stalks of celery, chopped
- 3 garlic cloves, minced
- 1 pkg. Hursts HamBeens Cajun 15 Bean Soup (with seasoning packet)
- 1 pkg. smoked sausage, sliced
- 1 (14-oz.) can diced tomatoes
- 3 c. beef broth
  Hot sauce, to taste
  Salt and pepper, to taste
  Rice (optional)

NOTE Add 8 c. water for Crock-Pot® Express.

Directions

SLOW

1. Rinse beans and place in a large bowl. Add enough water to cover the beans by about 5–6 inches. Soak overnight.
2. Drain beans and place in slow cooker. Set sausage aside and add remaining ingredients, including the Cajun seasoning packet to the slow cooker. Stir well to combine.
3. Cover and cook on LOW for 8 hours. In last hour, slice the sausage and brown in a skillet over medium-high heat. Transfer to cooker.
4. Once the beans are soft, remove about 1 c. of beans and transfer to a food processor or blender. Pulse to puree and return to cooker.
5. Stir all ingredients to combine. Taste, and add a bit of hot sauce if needed. Serve in a bowl as a stew or serve over rice.

FAST

1. Rinse beans and place in the Crock-Pot® Express along with water.
2. Seal lid and steam valve and cook on Beans setting for 30 minutes. Do a Natural Release for 10 minutes, then open steam vent. Carefully remove the lid. Drain any remaining water and give the beans a stir.
3. Set sausage aside and add remaining ingredients, including the Cajun seasoning packet to the slow cooker. Stir well to combine.
4. Add sausage and cover. Close steam vent. Cook on the Beans setting for 10 minutes. Natural Release for 10 minutes. Carefully remove lid. Season with salt, pepper and additional hot sauce.

If you love spice but your family doesn't, add the spice to your bowl of stew.

Denver
Bison Chili

Chili may as well be the reason why the slow cooker was invented.

YIELD 8 to 10 portions **I** **SLOW COOK TIME** 6 to 7 hours **I**
EXPRESS COOK TIME 40 minutes

Ingredients

1	lb. ground bison
	Salt and pepper, to taste
1	onion, chopped
2	t. minced garlic
2	t. ground cumin
¾	t. cayenne pepper
1–2	T. chili powder
1	poblano pepper, seeded and chopped
1	(14.5-oz.) cans diced tomatoes
1	(8-oz.) can diced green chilies
1	(15-oz.) cans chili beans
1	(14.5-oz.) cans kidney beans

NOTE Add 1 c. water for Crock-Pot® Express.

Directions

SLOW

1. Crumble raw bison into a 5-quart slow cooker.
2. Sprinkle meat with salt and pepper.
3. Place onions on top of the meat, followed by remaining seasonings and poblano pepper.
4. Next, add tomatoes, green chilies, chili beans and kidney beans. (Do not drain!)
5. Cover and cook on LOW for 6 to 7 hours.
6. Break up cooked meat with a wooden spoon and stir to incorporate into chili.
7. Taste and add additional seasonings as needed.

FAST

1. Crumble bison in the Crock-Pot® Express.
2. Sprinkle meat with salt and pepper. Place onions over top meat, followed by remaining seasonings and poblano pepper. Next, add tomatoes, green chilies, chili beans, kidney beans (do not drain!) and water.
3. Cook on Soup setting for 30 minutes, followed by a Natural Release for 10 minutes.
4. Break up cooked meat with a wooden spoon and stir to incorporate into chili.
5. Taste and add additional seasonings as needed.

Make it a dip by serving alongside tortilla chips, cheese and sour cream!

Soups

This soup is even better reheated the next day!

Split Pea and Sausage Soup

Not only is this soup hearty, it's also pretty lucky. Split peas are supposed to ensure you have a good new year!

YIELD 10 portions **I SLOW COOK TIME** 6 hours **I**
EXPRESS COOK TIME 33 minutes

Ingredients

1	lb. bulk pork sausage
1	(28-oz.) can crushed tomatoes
½	small head of cabbage, chopped
1	small onion, diced
32	oz. chicken broth
1	red bell pepper, chopped
1	t. garlic powder
	Salt and pepper to taste
1	lb. dried green split peas

NOTE Add 2 c. water for Crock-Pot® Express.

Directions

SLOW

1. Rinse and sort peas. Set aside.
2. In a large skillet at medium-high heat, cook sausage and onion together until cooked through.
3. Drain and add sausage mixture to a 6-quart slow cooker. Add the remaining ingredients. Stir well.
4. Cover and cook on LOW for 6 hours.
5. Once the beans are nice and soft, remove about 1 c. of beans and transfer to a food processor or blender. Pulse to puree and return to the slow cooker.
6. Stir all ingredients to combine. Taste, and add a bit of hot sauce if needed.
7. Serve in a bowl as a stew or serve over rice.

FAST

1. Rinse and sort peas. Set aside.
2. Heat Crock-Pot® Express on Sauté setting. Cook sausage and onions together. Drain grease.
3. Add water along with other ingredients.
4. Cover with lid and close steam vent. Cook on Soup setting for 18 minutes followed by 15 minutes Natural Release.

Lamb Stew

This succulent stew will quickly become a family favorite.

YIELD 6 portions **I** **SLOW COOK TIME** 7 to 8 hours **I**
EXPRESS COOK TIME 45 minutes

Ingredients

- 2 lb. lamb shoulder meat, cut in 1-inch cubes
- 1 T. chili powder
- 1 (4-oz.) can diced green chilies
- 1 (14.5-oz.) can diced tomatoes
- 3 c. chicken stock
- 1 large yellow onion, sliced
- 8 oz. mushrooms, quartered
- 1 T. minced garlic
- 2 T. red wine vinegar
- 2 t. oregano
- 1 t. pepper
- 1 t. sea salt
- 1 t. dried thyme
- ½ t. cardamon
- 1 t. ground cumin
- ½ c. chopped cilantro

Directions

SLOW

1. Place sliced onions in the bottom of a 6-quart slow cooker.
2. Place the cubed lamb on top of the onions.
3. In a medium bowl, combine chilies, diced tomatoes, garlic and seasonings. Pour over lamb in the slow cooker.
4. Add chicken stock and vinegar, then top with mushrooms.
5. Cover and cook on LOW for 7 to 8 hours.
6. Serve in bowls and garnish with freshly chopped cilantro.

FAST

1. Follow steps 1-4 of the SLOW recipe in a Crock-Pot® Express.
2. Cook on the Soup/Stew setting for 35 minutes followed by 10 minute Natural Release.
3. Serve in bowls and garnish with freshly chopped cilantro.

If you're not a lamb fan, swap it out for grass-fed beef.

Soups

Vegetarian
Barley Soup

A great sick-day remedy, this soup will help nurse you back to health.

YIELD 8 to 10 portions **I** **SLOW COOK TIME** 6 to 8 hours **I**
EXPRESS COOK TIME 40 minutes

Ingredients

- 2 T. oil
- 1 onion, sliced
- 1 t. salt
- ½ t. pepper
- 2 t. garlic powder
- 4 c. vegetable broth
- 6 c. water
- 1 (14.5 oz.) can petite diced tomatoes
- 4 stalks celery, chopped
- 4 carrots, chopped
- 6 green onions, chopped
- ½ c. fresh parsley, chopped
- 1 c. barley
- 1 t. dried thyme (optional)

Directions

SLOW

1. Heat oil in a skillet on medium-high and add onions, salt, pepper and garlic powder. Sauté until onions are almost translucent. Place onion mixture in large oval slow cooker. Deglaze with ¼ c. vegetable broth and transfer to slow cooker.
2. Add the rest of the broth, water, tomatoes, celery, carrots, green onions, parsley and barley to the cooker.
3. Cover and cook on LOW for 6 to 8 hours, or until the vegetables and barley are tender.
4. Add the thyme just before serving.

FAST

1. Pour oil in the Crock-Pot® Express and heat on the Sauté setting. Add onions, salt, pepper and garlic powder.
2. Sauté until onions are almost translucent.
3. Pour ¼ c. of the vegetable broth into the cooker and heat for a minute. Stir to scrape up the browned bits.
4. Add the rest of the broth, water, tomatoes, celery, carrots, green onions, parsley and barley to the cooker.
5. Cook on Soup/Stew setting for 35 minutes, followed by 5 minutes Natural Release. Add the thyme just before serving.

Feel free to add more of your favorite vegetables, like onions or zucchini.

Harvest
Chicken Soup

Warm up with this cozy homemade soup on chilly autumn evenings.

YIELD 6 to 8 portions **I** **SLOW COOK TIME** 4 to 6 hours **I**
EXPRESS COOK TIME 5 minutes

Ingredients

- 1 bay leaf
- 1 t. dried thyme, or 1 sprig fresh
  Freshly ground black pepper
- 4 c. chicken stock
- 1 whole bone-in rotisserie chicken breast, cooked and shredded
- 2 T. butter
- 2 carrots, peeled and chopped
- 3 celery stalks, washed and chopped
- 1 t. minced garlic
- ⅛ t. minced ginger
- 1 onion, chopped
- 1 zucchini, chopped
- 2 yellow squash, chopped
- 3 mushrooms, sliced
  Salt, to taste

NOTE Replace bouquet garni with 1 t. thyme and freshly ground black pepper for Crock-Pot® Express.

Directions

SLOW

1. Prepare a bouquet garni—take the bay leaf, sprig of thyme and peppercorns and tie in a piece of cheesecloth or a tea bag.
2. Prepare remaining ingredients and place in a slow cooker.
3. Add the bouquet garni to the soup.
4. Cover and cook on LOW for 6 hours or HIGH for 4 hours.
5. Remove bouquet garni before serving and enjoy!

FAST

1. Place all ingredients in a Crock-Pot® Express.
2. Cook 5 minutes on Soup setting; quick release the steam.

Soups

Chicken Noodle Soup

There's nothing like this classic bowl of soup to warm you up.

YIELD 8 to 10 portions **|** **SLOW COOK TIME** 8 hours **|**
EXPRESS COOK TIME 18 minutes

Ingredients

- 4 boneless, skinless chicken breasts
- 8 c. chicken broth
- 3 carrots, peeled and cut into ¼-in. slices
- 2 stalks of celery, cut into ¼-in. slices
- 1 medium onion, chopped
- 2 garlic cloves, minced
- 1 bay leaf
- ½ t. dried thyme
  Salt and pepper, to taste
- 3 c. wide egg noodles, uncooked

NOTE Add 2 T. butter for Crock-Pot® Express. If using thick chicken breasts, you may need to increase cooking time. Always ensure that chicken has reached an internal temperature of 165 degrees F before consuming.

Directions

SLOW

1. Combine broth, carrots, celery, onion, garlic, bay leaves, thyme, salt and pepper.
2. Set the chicken on the vegetables in the slow cooker.
3. Cover. and cook on LOW for 8 hours.
4. Remove chicken and shred (use two forks for easy shredding). Remove bay leaves and throw away.
5. Add noodles to the slow cooker and cook for 20 minutes.
6. Return shredded chicken to the soup and combine well.
7. Serve in bowls with saltine crackers.

FAST

1. Place 2 T. Butter in the Crock-Pot® Express on the Sauté setting.
2. Add onion, garlic, carrots and celery. Stir and sauté for 3 minutes or until onion is tender.
3. Place chicken in the cooker and top with broth, thyme, salt and pepper. Add bay leaf.
4. Cover and lock lid. Close steam vent. Cook on Soup setting for 8 minutes, followed by a natural release for 10 minutes.
5. Remove chicken and set aside. Remove bay leaf and throw away.
6. Add noodles to the cooker and turn to sauté setting. Cook for 6 minutes or until soft.
7. Meanwhile. shred or chop chicken and return it to the soup. Stir and serve.

Corn and Red Pepper Chowder

Your friends and family will be chowin' down on this dish, so make sure you have seconds ready.

YIELD 5 to 6 portions I **SLOW COOK TIME** 8 hours 30 minutes to 10 hours 30 minutes I **EXPRESS COOK TIME** 10 minutes

Ingredients

- 1 yellow onion, finely diced
- 1 large red bell pepper, seeded and diced
- 3 medium potatoes, peeled and diced
- 4 c. sweet corn kernels, frozen, divided (or approx. 4 ears of fresh corn)
- 1 t. ground cumin
- ½ t. smoked paprika
- ⅛ t. cayenne pepper
- 1 t. kosher salt
- 4 c. chicken broth
- 1 c. milk or half-and-half
     Freshly ground pepper, to taste
     Extra veggies and sour cream, to garnish

NOTE Add 1 T. olive oil to Fast ingredients.

Directions

SLOW

1. Place the onion, red pepper, potatoes, 1 c. of the corn, cumin, smoked paprika, cayenne pepper,and salt in a 6-quart slow cooker.
2. Pour broth over top and cover. Cook on LOW for 8 to 10 hours.
3. Use an immersion blender to puree the soup. Remove 1 c. of soup and pour into a medium bowl. Stir in the milk into the cup of soup and then pour the soup back into the slow cooker.
4. Add remaining corn to the cooker and cover. Cook on LOW for another 30 minutes. Season with salt and pepper, to taste.

FAST

1. Heat olive oil in the Crock-Pot® Express on Sauté setting. Sauté the onion 3 minutes or until soft.
2. Add the red pepper, potatoes, 1 c. corn, cumin, smoked paprika, cayenne pepper and salt. Pour broth over top.
3. Cover and lock lid; close steam vent. Cook on Soup setting for 10 minutes. Do a Natural Release and carefully remove lid.
4. Use an immersion blender to puree the soup. Remove 1 c. soup and pour into a medium bowl. Stir in the milk/half-and-half into the cup of soup and pour the soup back into the cooker.
5. Add remaining corn to pot. Turn on Sauté setting and stir, cooking uncovered until heated through. Season with salt and pepper.

Soups

Sub the noodles out for crusty bread if you're looking to make this meal less filling!

Steak Diane Mushroom Stew

Serve up your steak stew-style in this easy recipe.

YIELD 6 portions **I** **SLOW COOK TIME** 4 to 10 hours **I**
EXPRESS COOK TIME 30 minutes

Ingredients

1½ lb. beef round steak, boneless,
    cut in 1-in. cubes
2   medium onions, cut in wedges
2   garlic cloves, minced
3   c. fresh button mushrooms,
    sliced
1   (10¾-oz.) can golden
    mushroom soup, condensed
¼   c. tomato paste
2   t. Worcestershire sauce
1   t. dry mustard
½   t. black pepper, cracked
3   c. hot cooked noodles

Directions

SLOW

1. Place onions topped with garlic
   and mushrooms in a 3½- to
   4-quart slow cooker.
2. Transfer steak on top of the
   onions and mushrooms.
3. In a separate bowl combine the
   remaining ingredients except the
   noodles and stir well. Pour over
   the steak in the cooker.
4. Cover and cook on LOW for 8 to
   10 hours or on HIGH for 4 to 5
   hours.
5. Serve with noodles, prepared
   according to package
   instructions.

FAST

1. Heat 1 T. oil in the Crock-Pot®
   Express on the Sauté setting.
   Add onions and garlic and sauté
   for 3 minutes.
2. Add steak and season with salt
   and pepper. Cook just long
   enough to brown—about 2
   minutes, stirring frequently. Add
   mushrooms and turn off cooker.
3. In a separate bowl combine the
   remaining ingredients except
   the noodles and stir well. Pour
   over steak.
4. Cover and lock lid; close steam
   vent. Cook on Soup setting for
   30 minutes followed by a quick
   release of the steam.
5. Prepare noodles, before
   serving, according to
   directions on package.

If desired, leave the potato skins on. They're chock-full of vitamins and fiber!

Smashed
Potato Soup

Put your recipe for Loaded Potato Soup down and try this smashing alternative.

YIELD 8 portions I **SLOW COOK TIME** 6 hours 30 minutes to 8 hours 30 minutes I **EXPRESS COOK TIME** 20 minutes

Ingredients

3 lb. potatoes, diced, peeled if desired

1 yellow onion, diced

2 green chiles, peeled, deseeded and chopped

1 t. minced garlic
 Salt and pepper to taste

32 oz. chicken broth

½ c. sour cream

4 oz. frozen broccoli

12 oz. sharp cheddar cheese, shredded

4 green onions, sliced

12 pieces cooked bacon, crumbled

NOTE Add 2 T. butter to Fast ingredients.

Directions

SLOW

1. Place diced potatoes, yellow onion, chilies, garlic, salt, pepper and chicken broth in a 6-quart slow cooker.
2. Cover and cook on LOW for 6 to 8 hours.
3. Carefully use a hand blender and slightly whip soup to break up potatoes into smaller pieces.
4. Add sour cream, broccoli and cheese. Stir to combine.
5. Cover and cook for an additional 30 minutes on LOW.
6. Top with bacon, green onions and cheese when serving.

FAST

1. Heat Crock-Pot® Express on Sauté (High) setting; add butter. Once butter is melted, add onions, garlic, salt and pepper; sauté 2 to 3 minutes. Add potatoes, chilies and broth.
2. Cover and cook on Soup setting for 10 minutes. Natural release steam for 5 minutes; then open valve.
3. Carefully use a hand blender and slightly whip soup to break up potatoes into smaller pieces. Do this in batches, if necessary.
4. Add sour cream, cheese and broccoli. Stir to combine.
5. Cover and cook on Sauté setting for an additional 5 minutes. Top with bacon, green onions and cheese when serving.

Soups

Creamy
Shrimp Bisque

This bisque also makes a great appetizer.

Rich and luxurious, this soup will hit the spot.

YIELD 4 portions | **SLOW COOK TIME** 3 to 4 hours | **EXPRESS COOK TIME** 11 minutes

Ingredients

- 2   T. butter or margarine
- 1   c. mushrooms, sliced
- 2   T. green onion, sliced
- 1   garlic clove
- 14 oz. chicken broth
- ¼   c. tomato paste
- 3   T. flour, all purpose
- ½   c. light cream
- 1   lb. frozen shrimp, thawed shelled and deveined
- ½   c. dry white wine (like Chablis)
- 1   T. chopped, fresh parsley

NOTE Use fresh, raw, deveined shrimp instead of frozen for Crock-Pot® Express.

Directions

SLOW

1. In a large skillet, melt the butter or margarine and add the mushrooms, green onion and garlic until translucent, stirring occasionally.
2. Add the broth and tomato paste just to warm through a little.
3. In a separate cup, stir together the flour and cream until well blended and smooth.
4. Stir into broth mixture.
5. Transfer to a 3½- to 4-quart slow cooker.
6. Cover and cook on LOW for 3 to 4 hours.
7. If your bisque is thin, add a few teaspoons of cornstarch or flour to cold water. Whisk thoroughly to get rid of lumps and add to bisque.
8. About 30 minutes before your bisque is done, add the wine and shrimp, and stir into the bisque. Cover, and continue to cook for the last 30 minutes.
9. Sprinkle parsley and additional shrimp (if desire) on bisque in serving bowls.

FAST

1. Press Sauté function to heat the Crock-Pot® Express. Add butter.
2. Once butter is melted, add the mushrooms, green onion and garlic until translucent, stirring occasionally. Add the tomato paste and stir for 1 minute. Add the flour and stir well to combine.
3. Pour in the wine and use a wooden spoon to deglaze the pot. Add the broth and stir well.
4. Cover with lid and seal steam vent. Cook on Soup setting for 1 minute (you'll have to press cancel after one minute) followed by a quick pressure release.
5. Stir in cream and shrimp.
6. Cover and keep cooker on the warm setting for 10 minutes.
7. Garnish with parsley when serving.

Save those Shells...

...to make your own shrimp stock! Add the shells, 8 c. water, a bay leaf and a few peppercorns in the slow cooker or multi-cooker. Slow cook for 8 hours or pressure cook for 45 minutes. Strain the stock and freeze in 2-c. portions for future seafood bisques.

Tortilla Soup

With its crunchy texture and flavorful taste, this soup will become a family favorite.

YIELD 8 portions I **SLOW COOK TIME** 7 to 8 hours I
EXPRESS COOK TIME 22 minutes

Ingredients

- 2   chicken breast halves, boneless, skinless and cubed
- 1   onion, finely chopped
- 1   garlic clove, crushed
- 3   medium tomatoes, peeled and chopped
- 4   c. chicken broth
- ¼   t. salt
- ⅛   t. pepper
- 1   mild green chile, seeded and chopped
- 2   T. vegetable oil
- 4   corn tortillas, halved and cut into ¼-in. strips
     Shredded Monterey Jack cheese, for topping
- 2   T. chopped fresh cilantro
- 2   T. choppe, fresh parsley

NOTE Cut chicken breasts in half for Crock-Pot® Express.

Directions

SLOW

1. In a 6-quart slow cooker, combine chicken breasts, onion, garlic, tomatoes, broth, salt, pepper and green chile.
2. Cover and cook on LOW for 7 to 8 hours.
3. Remove chicken breasts and shred with two forks or shredding claws and transfer back to cooker and stir in soup. Cover to keep it hot!
4. In large skillet, heat oil and add tortilla strips. Cook, stirring, over medium heat until crisp; drain on paper towels.
5. Ladle tortilla soup into bowls. Place 1 or 2 T. of shredded Monterey Jack cheese in each serving bowl, if desired. Top with tortilla strips and parsley.

FAST

1. Blend onion, garlic, tomatoes and green chile together in a blender or food processor.
2. Using the Sauté setting, heat oil in the Crock-Pot® Express. Add blended ingredients plus salt and pepper. Sauté 10 minutes or until thickened.
3. Add chicken, broth and tortillas.
4. Cover with lid. Close steam vent. Cook on Soup setting for 22 minutes followed by a quick pressure release.
5. Remove chicken breasts and shred with two forks or shredding claws. Transfer back to multi-cooker and stir in soup.
6. Serve soup topped with shredded cheese, tortilla chips and parsley.

Soups

Veal Stew

This stew is so tender that the potatoes and veal will be easier to slice through than butter.

YIELD 4 portions | **SLOW COOK TIME** 7 to 8 hours |
EXPRESS COOK TIME 25 minutes

Ingredients

- 2   T. coconut oil
- 2   T. flour
-     Salt, to taste
- ¼   t. black pepper
- 1   lb. veal shoulder, cubed
- ½   c. beef broth, divided
- 5   carrots, peeled and chopped
- 1   red bell pepper, cut in strips
- 1   large onion, chopped
- 2   garlic cloves, minced
- 1   (14½-oz.) can diced tomatoes
- ¼   t. ground sage
- ¼   t. dried oregano, crushed

Directions

SLOW

1. Heat coconut oil in a large skillet over medium-high heat.
2. Mix flour, salt and pepper in a shallow dish.
3. Dredge the veal through the flour mixture and sear on both sides until there is a nice brown finish. Remove veal to plate.
4. Carefully, pour ¼ c. of the beef broth into the hot skillet, scraping up any browned bits. Transfer to slow cooker, if using.
5. Place carrots in cooker and put browned veal on top of carrots.
6. Next, add the remaining beef broth, peppers, onion, garlic and diced tomatoes to the slow cooker. Top with the sage and oregano.
7. Cover and cook on LOW for 7 to 8 hours.

FAST

1. Heat coconut oil in the Crock-Pot® Express on Sauté setting.
2. Mix flour, salt and pepper in a shallow dish. Dredge the veal through the flour mixture and add to the pot.
3. Sear on both sides just until there is a nice brown finish, about 30 seconds per side. Remove from pot and set aside.
4. Add onions and garlic. Sauté just until soft, about 3-5 minutes. Add ¼ c. of broth to deglaze the pot, scraping and stirring with a wooden spoon. Add remaining broth, diced tomatoes, carrots, the browned veal and seasonings.
5. Cover with lid and seal steam vent. Cook on Soup setting for 15 minutes. Natural Release pressure for 10 minutes then open steam vent. Remove lid and allow stew to sit for 5 minutes before serving.

Tortellini Squash Stew

Creamy and comforting, this tasty stew is the perfect remedy to a gloomy day.

YIELD 6 portions I **SLOW COOK TIME** 6 to 7 hours I
EXPRESS COOK TIME 20 minutes

Ingredients

1	large onion, diced
¾	t. salt
	Pepper, to taste
2	lb. butternut squash, peeled, seeded and cubed
2	medium zucchini, chopped
2	medium yellow summer squash, chopped
1	large red bell pepper, seeded and diced
1	(28-oz.) can crushed tomatoes
1	(14.5-oz.) pkg. chicken broth
1	T. dried oregano
1	t. garlic powder
9	oz. fresh/refrigerated cheese tortellini
5	oz. baby spinach
3	T. Parmesan cheese, grated

Directions

SLOW

1. Heat oil over medium-high in large skillet; add onions and salt and sauté until translucent. Transfer to slow cooker.
2. Top onions with squash, zucchini, yellow summer squash, pepper, tomatoes, broth, oregano, garlic powder and pepper.
3. Cover and cook on LOW for 6 to 7 hours.
4. Remove lid and stir in tortellini.
5. Cover and cook for 15 to 20 minutes, or until pasta is cooked to al dente. Uncover and gently stir in spinach and Parmesan.
6. Cover and cook for about 5 minutes or until spinach wilts.

FAST

1. Heat oil on Sauté setting in the Crock-Pot® Express. Add onions and cook until translucent.
2. Top onions with butternut squash, zucchini, yellow summer squash, pepper, tomatoes, broth, oregano, garlic powder, salt and pepper.
3. Cover and cook on Soup setting for 5 minutes. Do a Natural Release for 10 minutes.
4. Remove lid and stir in tortellini, spinach and Parmesan.
5. Cover and cook on Sauté setting for 5 minutes, or until pasta is cooked to al dente.

Soups

Savory
Turkey and Dumplings

Thanks to this recipe, making dumplings has never been so easy.

YIELD 4 to 6 portions I **SLOW COOK TIME** 4 hours 30 minutes to
7 hours I **EXPRESS COOK TIME** 20 minutes

Ingredients

- 2 c. cooked turkey, roughly chopped
- ½ c. diced onion
- 2 celery ribs, chopped
- ½ c. diced carrots
- 1 (14.5-oz.) can petite diced tomatoes
- 1 T. poultry seasoning
- 12 oz. condensed cream of chicken soup
- 2½ c. chicken broth
- 1 (8-oz.) can crescent roll dough or biscuit dough

NOTE Add 2 T. oil for Crock-Pot® Express.

Directions

SLOW

1. Add turkey and vegetables to cooker. Season with salt and poultry seasoning. Cover all with condensed soup and broth.
2. Cover and cook on LOW for 4 to 6 hours.
3. Meanwhile, form raw dough into small balls.
4. Add dough balls to top of the soup mixture after 4 to 6 hour mark. Cover and cook on HIGH another 30 to 60 minutes, or until dough is cooked.

FAST

1. Heat oil on Sauté setting in the Crock-Pot® Express. Add onions, celery and carrots; cook for 5 minutes.
2. Add turkey and tomatoes to crock. Season with salt and poultry seasoning. Pour in soup and broth.
3. Form dough into 1½-in. balls and place on top.
4. Cover and lock lid into place. Close steam vent. Cook on Soup setting for 10 minutes. Do a natural release of the steam for 10 minutes then carefully remove lid.
5. Gently stir before serving.

Chicken and Wild Rice Soup

One bowl of this warm, comforting soup will fill you up.

YIELD 10 portions **I** **SLOW COOK TIME** 7 to 8 hours **I**
EXPRESS COOK TIME 15 minutes

Ingredients

- 1   c. wild rice, uncooked, rinsed
- 1   lb. boneless, skinless chicken breasts
- 2   ribs of celery, washed and chopped
- 1   medium onion, chopped
- 2   carrots, peeled and chopped
- 4   oz. sliced mushrooms
- 1   (48-oz.) pkg. chicken stock
- 1   t. thyme
- 1   t. sage
- ½   c. unsalted butter
- ¾   c. all-purpose flour
- 2   c. milk
- 3   T. white wine

Directions

SLOW

1. Transfer the wild rice, chicken, celery, onions, carrots, mushrooms, chicken stock and seasonings into a 6-quart slow cooker. Cover and cook on LOW for 7 to 8 hours.
2. Carefully remove chicken from the slow cooker and shred with forks. Transfer the shredded chicken back to the cooker.
3. When wild rice and chicken are done cooking, melt butter in a saucepan. Gently add in flour and let mixture bubble for 1 minute.
4. Slowly whisk in the milk until a thick, creamy mixture forms. Stir in the wine. Mix this with the rice and chicken, stirring to combine.

FAST

1. Add oil to the cooker and press the Sauté button. Once oil is heated, add the celery, onions and carrots. Sauté 5 minutes.
2. Add rice and stir well. Next, stir in mushrooms then add chicken, stock and seasonings.
3. Cover and lock lid. Close steam vent. Cook on Soup setting for 5 minutes. Do a Natural Release for 10 minutes
4. Carefully remove chicken and shred with forks. Transfer the shredded chicken back to the cooker.
5. When the wild rice and chicken are done cooking, melt the butter in a saucepan. Gently add in the flour and stir until incorporated. Let the mixture bubble for 1 minute.
6. Slowly whisk in the milk until a thick, creamy mixture forms. Stir in the wine. Add this to the soup and stir well to combine.

Mains

After you master these mains, your family will dash to the table every night of the week.

Nothing beats a good rack of ribs!

Spicy
Steak Fajitas

These flavorful fajitas are so good they will become a dinnertime staple.

YIELD 8 portions **I** **SLOW COOK TIME** 4 hours **I**
EXPRESS COOK TIME 7 minutes

Ingredients

- 1 (7-oz.) can chipotle peppers in adobo sauce
  Juice of two limes
- ¼ c. plus 2 T. olive oil, divided
- 1 flank steak
- 1 red bell pepper, sliced
- 1 yellow bell pepper, sliced
- 1 onion, chopped (yellow or red)
  Shredded lettuce, to serve
  Cotija cheese, to serve
  Flour tortillas, to serve

Directions

SLOW

1. Place chipotles in adobo sauce in the blender with the juice of two limes and ¼ c. olive oil and puree.
2. Put the flank steak in a gallon sized plastic bag. Pour marinade over top.
3. Seal bag and refrigerate steak. Marinate overnight.
4. Place onion and peppers in a 6-quart slow cooker. Place steak AND marinade on top of peppers and onions. Cover and cook on LOW for 4 hours.

5. When steak is finished, remove from slow cooker and let sit for 15 minutes on a wood cutting board.
6. For best results, slice steak diagonally after it's had time to rest. Serve steak in warm tortillas and top with peppers, onions, lettuce and cotija cheese.

FAST

1. Follow steps 1-3 of the SLOW recipe.
2. Heat 2 T. oil in the Crock-Pot® Express on the Sauté setting. Add onion, followed by peppers and sauté for 2 minutes.
3. Place steak and marinade on top of peppers and onions.
4. Cover and cook on Beans/ Chili setting (High Pressure) for 6 minutes. When steak is finished, do a Natural Release for 1 minute, then carefully turn the steam to open and vent.
5. Remove the steak from the slow cooker and let sit for 15 minutes on a wood cutting board.
6. Follow step 6 of SLOW recipe.

Main Meals

Tequila Lime Chicken

Chicken so juicy and flavorful that you might not be able to go back to any other marinade.

YIELD 4 portions **I SLOW COOK TIME** 7 to 8 hours **I**
EXPRESS COOK TIME 11 minutes

Ingredients

- 4 boneless, skinless chicken breasts
- ½ c. orange juice
- Juice of one lime
- 1 T. chili powder
- 1 t. ground cumin
- 1 (4-oz.) can mild green chiles
- 1 T. minced garlic
- 2 oz. tequila

Directions

SLOW

1. Place chicken in a 4-quart slow cooker.
2. Combine remaining ingredients in a small bowl and place over top chicken.
3. Cover and cook on LOW for 7 to 8 hours.

FAST

1. Cut chicken breasts into thirds and place in a single layer in the Crock-Pot® Express.
2. Combine remaining ingredients in a small bowl and place on top of chicken.
3. Cover, seal steam vent and cook on Beans/Chili setting for 6 minutes, followed by a Natural Release for 5 minutes.
4. Carefully remove chicken from pot. Let rest a few minutes before cutting.

Freeze It

With how busy life can be, it's sometimes hard to get dinner on the table. When I know I have a packed schedule, I prep the ingredients a few nights before and then I stick everything in the freezer, so on the day I want to prepare a meal, I can just put everything in the slow cooker!

Cincinnati Chili

The allspice and cinnamon gives this chili its signature flavor.

YIELD 6 portions **I SLOW COOK TIME** 7 to 9 hours **I**
EXPRESS COOK TIME 10 minutes

Ingredients

1½	lb. lean ground beef
2	onions, chopped
6	garlic cloves, minced
2	stalks celery, chopped
2	T. chili powder
1	T. smoked paprika
1	T. Italian seasoning
1	t. ground cinnamon
½	t. cayenne pepper
1	t. ground cumin
½	t. crushed red pepper flakes
¼	t. ground allspice
½	t. salt
½	t. black pepper
2	14.5-oz. cans diced tomatoes
8	oz. can tomato sauce
½	c. water
	Julienned red pepper, for garnish

You can also add a can of beans for extra fiber!

Directions

SLOW

1. In a large skillet, brown ground beef, onions and garlic. Transfer to paper towel-lined plate to absorb any grease.
2. Place beef mixture and all remaining ingredients into 6-quart slow cooker and stir.
3. Cover and cook on LOW for 6 hours. Serve over spaghetti or as a hot dog topping.

FAST

1. Heat oil in Crock-Pot® Express over the Sauté setting. Add ground beef, onions and garlic. Cook just until beef has a bit of pink remaining.
2. Transfer to paper towel lined plate to absorb any grease. Place beef mixture back in the pot along with all remaining ingredients.
3. Cover with lid and close steam vent. Cook on Soup setting (High Pressure) for 10 minutes followed by a quick release. Serve over spaghetti or as a hot dog topping.

Cran-Orange Pork Loin

This zesty mix of cranberries and oranges will liven up your dinner table.

YIELD 6 to 8 portions | **SLOW COOK TIME** 7 to 8 hours |
EXPRESS COOK TIME 13 minutes

Ingredients

- 1 large onion, chopped
- 3 lb. pork loin roast
- 2 cups cranberries
- 1 c. fresh squeezed orange juice
- 1 T. orange zest
- 1 T. spicy mustard
- Salt and pepper, to taste
- ¼ t. allspice

NOTE Add 2 T. oil for Crock-Pot® Express.

Directions

SLOW

1. Place onion, then pork in a 5- to 6-quart slow cooker. Top with remaining ingredients.
2. Cover and cook on LOW for 7 to 8 hours.
3. Remove pork and let sit for 5 minutes. Slice, then top with sauce/cranberries from slow cooker and garnish with an orange slice for serving.

FAST

1. Heat oil in the Crock-Pot® Express on the Sauté setting.

When oil is hot, add pork and sear on all sides. Set aside.
2. Next, add onion and sauté for 2 minutes, or until softened. Place the pork on the onions and top with remaining ingredients.
3. Cover with the lid and seal the steam vent. Cook on Meat/Stew setting (High Pressure), but turn off the cooker at 3 minutes.
4. Naturally Release pressure for 10 minutes, then carefully remove lid. Remove pork and test temperature with a meat thermometer; it should read 160 degrees F.
5. Allow it to rest for 5 minutes, then slice. Serve with sauce/cranberries from the cooker and garnish with an orange slice.

If you don't have time to squeeze some orange juice fresh, a carton of orange juice works too!

Healthier
Chicken Curry

This dish is basically made for the slow cooker because it's at its best and most tender when cooked "low and slow."

YIELD 6 portions **I SLOW COOK TIME** 7 to 8 hours **I**
EXPRESS COOK TIME 10 minutes

Ingredients

- 1.5 lb. boneless, skinless chicken breast or thighs, cubed
- 1 (6-oz.) can tomato paste
- 1½ c. tomato sauce
- 1 (13½-oz.) can lite coconut milk
- 1 small onion, diced
- ½ green bell pepper, seeded and chopped
- 1 c. green peas
- 2 T. curry powder
- 1 t. garlic salt
- ½ t. crushed red pepper
- 1 T. honey

NOTE Add ½ c. chicken broth for Crock-Pot® Express.

You could also cook the chicken breast whole, shred and then incorporate it back into the sauce.

Directions

SLOW
1. Place all ingredients in a 5-quart slow cooker and stir well to combine.
2. Cover and cook on LOW for 7 to 8 hours.
3. Serve over rice for a delicious meal!

FAST
1. Place all ingredients except the coconut milk in the Crock-Pot® Express and stir well to combine.
2. Cover and lock lid. Close steam vent. Cook on Soup setting (High Pressure) for 5 minutes. Do a quick release of steam and remove lid.
3. Stir in coconut milk. Set cooker to Sauté setting and cook, for 5 minutes, or until sauce is thickened.
4. Serve over rice for a delicious meal!

Main Meals

Instead of mincing onion, slice it and place it on top of the gravy mixture. ....▶

Creamy Mushroom Round Steak

Smothered in a creamy mushroom sauce, this steak is the definition of savory.

YIELD 2 to 4 portions **I SLOW COOK TIME** 7 to 9 hours **I EXPRESS COOK TIME** 10 minutes

Ingredients

1-2 lb. round steak

1 (10¾-oz.) can cream of mushroom soup

1 packet brown gravy mix

2 T. dried minced onion

2 carrots, chopped

2 potatoes, cut into chunks

¼ c. water

4 oz. mushrooms

Salt and pepper, to taste

Directions

SLOW

1. Spray a 5-6 quart slow cooker with nonstick cooking spray or coat with butter.
2. Place the round steak on the bottom of the cooker.
3. Combine the soup, brown gravy, onion, carrots, potatoes water and mushrooms in a bowl and pour over the steak.
4. Cover and cook on LOW for 7 to 9 hours.

FAST

1. Heat oil in the Crock-Pot® Express on the Sauté setting. Add onions and sauté for 2 minutes.
2. Add carrots and potatoes seasoned with salt and pepper. Stir and sauté for 2 minutes.
3. Place the round steak on top of veggies in the cooker.
4. Combine the soup, brown gravy, water and mushrooms in a bowl and pour over the steak
5. Cover and lock lid; close steam vent. Cook on Soup setting for 8 minutes. Turn off cooker. Natural Release the steam for 2 minutes, then do a full quick release.
6. Remove steak and let it rest before slicing. Serve steak topped with veggies and gravy from the cooker.

Spaghetti Squash with Pesto

A dish that's so good you won't even notice the noodles are made out of squash.

YIELD 2 to 3 portions **I** **SLOW COOK TIME** 4 hours **I**
EXPRESS COOK TIME 8 minutes

Ingredients

- 1 spaghetti squash
- ½ c. water
  Salt and pepper, to taste
- 1 tomato, seeded and diced (optional)
- 1 c. pesto sauce, plus more to taste

Directions

SLOW

1. Wash and dry squash. Cut in half lengthwise. Scoop out seeds and strings.
2. Place squash halves side by side in a 6-quart slow cooker.
3. Pour water around squash. Cover and cook on LOW for 4 hours.
4. Carefully remove squash (it will be hot!) and use a fork to scrape into a bowl. It will create "noodles" as you scrape.
5. Season lightly with sea salt and freshly ground pepper.
6. Add diced tomato, if desired, and pesto. Toss lightly.
7. Serve immediately, or refrigerate in a covered container for a cold "pasta" salad type dish.

FAST

1. Wash and dry squash. Cut squash in half lengthwise. Scoop out seeds and strings.
2. Pour 1 c. water in the bottom of the Crock-Pot® Express. Place a trivet on top and add squash.
3. Cover, lock lid and close steam vent. Cook on Soup setting for 8 minutes.
4. Carefully remove the squash (it will be hot!) and use a fork to scrape insides into a bowl. It will create "noodles" as you scrape. Season lightly with sea salt and freshly ground pepper.
5. Add diced tomato, if desired, and pesto sauce. Toss lightly.
6. Serve immediately, or refrigerate in a covered container for a cold "pasta" salad type dish.

Add pine nuts as a garnish for some extra crunch!

Main Meals

Balsamic Tomato Chicken

This spin on Italian chicken is delicious served over fresh pasta or with crusty bread!

YIELD 4 portions **I SLOW COOK TIME** 4 to 5 hours **I**
EXPRESS COOK TIME 10 minutes

Ingredients

- 1   onion
    Salt and pepper, to taste
- 4   boneless, skinless chicken breasts
- 1   (14.5-oz.) can diced tomatoes
- ⅓   c. balsamic vinegar
- 1   T. Italian seasoning
- 1   t. garlic salt
    Fresh mozzarella, torn into chunks (optional)

NOTE Add ¼ c. water for Crock-Pot® Express.

Directions

SLOW

1. Slice onion and place in the bottom of a slow cooker.
2. Season onion with salt and pepper and drizzle with olive oil.
3. Place chicken on top of onions.
4. In a small bowl, combine diced tomatoes, balsamic vinegar, Italian seasoning and garlic salt.
5. Pour tomato mixture over chicken.
6. Cover and cook on LOW for 4 to 5 hours.
7. If desired, dot with fresh mozzarella pieces, cover and cook on LOW for 20 additional minutes.

FAST

1. Heat oil in Crock-Pot® Express on the Sauté setting. Slice onion and place in the bottom of the cooker. Season onion with salt and pepper. Sauté for 2 minutes.
2. Place chicken on top of onions.
3. In a small bowl, combine water, diced tomatoes, balsamic vinegar, Italian seasoning and garlic salt.
4. Pour tomato mixture over chicken.
5. Cover and cook on Multigrain setting (High Pressure) for 10 minutes. Quick release steam.
6. Optional: Dot with fresh mozzarella pieces, cover and cook on Sauté/Low for 5 minutes. Serve over starch of your choice and enjoy!

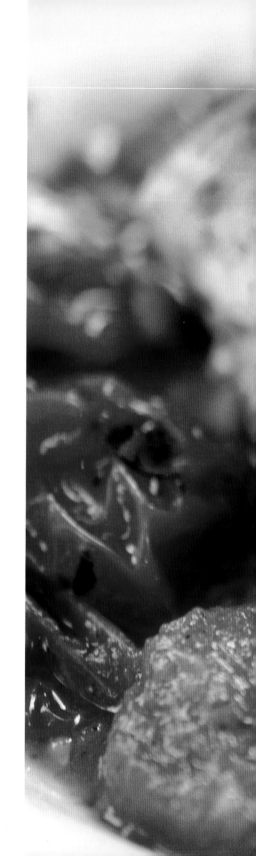

They're perfect on-the-go meals! Just wrap a few in foil and you're on your way.

Chicken Parmesan Sliders

These mouthwatering sliders will be a hit at any get-together.

YIELD 6 portions **I** **SLOW COOK TIME** 4 hours **I**
EXPRESS COOK TIME 10 minutes

Ingredients

- 4 boneless, skinless chicken breasts
- 2 c. marinara sauce
  Salt and pepper, to taste
- 1 t. garlic powder
- 2 t. sugar
- 1 T. Italian seasoning
- ¼ c. freshly grated Parmesan cheese
- 12 slices mozzarella cheese
- 12 slider rolls

Directions

SLOW

1. Place chicken breasts in a 5-quart slow cooker.
2. In a small bowl, combine marinara sauce, all the seasonings, sugar and Parmesan cheese.
3. Pour sauce mixture over chicken in the slow cooker.
4. Cover and cook on LOW for 4 hours.
5. Remove only the chicken from the slow cooker and shred with two forks.
6. Place shredded chicken back in the cooker set to WARM and stir to combine well with sauce.
7. To serve, split open slider rolls and place in a toaster oven to warm.
8. Top warmed slider rolls with shredded chicken and top with a slice of mozzarella cheese.

FAST

1. In a small bowl, combine marinara sauce, all the seasonings, sugar and Parmesan cheese.
2. Pour sauce mixture into Crock-Pot® Express and add chicken on top. Spoon some of the sauce over the chicken.
3. Cover and lock lid. Close steam vent. Cook on Multigrain setting for 10 minutes. Do a quick release of the steam.
4. Remove only the chicken from the pot and shred with a meat claw or two forks.
5. Place shredded chicken back in the cooker. Set to WARM and stir to combine well with sauce.
6. To serve, split open slider rolls and place in a toaster oven to warm. Top warmed slider rolls with shredded chicken and a slice of mozzarella cheese.

Main Meals

Veggie Lasagna with Alfredo

Vegetarian-friendly and delicious, this recipe breaks the rules (to delicious effect)!

YIELD 8 to 10 portions I **SLOW COOK TIME** 4 to 5 hours I **EXPRESS COOK TIME** 30 minutes

Ingredients

- ½   small red onion, chopped
- 2   c. fresh baby spinach
- 2   t. minced garlic
- 1¼ c. shredded carrots
- 1   small zucchini
- 6   oz. mushrooms
- 1   (14.5-oz.) can diced tomatoes, drained
- 1   T. Italian seasoning
- 1   t. garlic powder
- 1   egg
- 10 oz. whole milk ricotta cheese
- 1   t. dried parsley
- ½   t. freshly ground pepper
- 6   no-cook lasagna noodles
- 2   c. shredded mozzarella cheese
- ⅓   c. whole milk
- 1½ c. Alfredo sauce

Directions

SLOW

1. Place onions in a skillet over medium heat and sauté with the garlic. Add spinach and cover pan with lid. Stir once or twice then recover with lid.
2. In a separate bowl, combine zucchini, carrots, tomatoes and chopped mushrooms. Stir in sautéed spinach, onion and garlic.
3. Sprinkle Italian Seasoning over veggies and stir well. Set vegetables aside.
4. Whisk together Alfredo sauce with milk in a small bowl.
5. In another bowl, combine ricotta, egg, garlic powder, pepper and parsley.
6. Grease a 6-quart slow cooker with nonstick spray.
7. Make 2 layers with ingredients in this order: ½ c. Alfredo sauce, 3 noodles (break to fit), ⅓ of the ricotta mixture, ⅓ of veggie mixture and 1 c. of mozzarella.
8. After the second layer, pour the rest of the Alfredo sauce on top of lasagna.
9. Cover and cook on LOW for 4 to 5 hours.

FAST

1. Heat oil in the Crock-Pot® Express over the Sauté setting. Place onions and garlic in heated pot. Cook 2 to 3 minutes or until softened.
2. Reduce Sauté setting to LOW. Add spinach and cover pan with lid. Stir a few times then recover.
3. Thinly slice zucchini and chop mushrooms. In a separate bowl, combine zucchini, carrots, tomatoes and mushrooms.
4. Stir in sautéed spinach, onion and garlic. Turn off cooker. Sprinkle Italian seasoning over veggies and stir well. Set vegetables aside.
5. Whisk together Alfredo sauce with milk in a small bowl. In another bowl, combine ricotta cheese, egg, garlic powder, pepper and parsley.
6. Grease a 7-in. springform pan with nonstick spray.
7. Make 2 layers with ingredients in this order: ½ c. Alfredo sauce, 3 noodles (break to fit), ⅓ of the ricotta mixture, ⅓ of veggie mixture and 1 c. of mozzarella. After the second layer, pour the rest of the Alfredo sauce on top of the lasagna.
8. Pour 1 c. water in cooker. Place trivet inside. Cover lasagna tightly with foil and place on trivet. Cook for 20 minutes on Multigrain setting followed by a 10 minute quick release. Remove foil and let cool slightly before serving.

Smoking your ribs
with a smoke
infuser adds a
lot of flavor.

Hickory Smoked
BBQ Ribs

Skip the grill and cook up these BBQ ribs in your slow cooker, so you can have them any time of year!

YIELD 4 to 6 portions I **SLOW COOK TIME** 8 hours I
EXPRESS COOK TIME 30 minutes

Ingredients

- 3   lb. rack of pork ribs
- 2   t. seasoning salt
- 2   t. garlic powder
- ½   c. brown sugar
- 1   t. smoked paprika
- ½   c. BBQ sauce

SPECIAL EQUIPMENT
Handheld smoke infuser

NOTE Add 2 c. apple cider or juice for Crock-Pot® Express.

Directions

SLOW
1. Cut rack of pork ribs in half and place both halves side by side in a large slow cooker.
2. Mix dry seasonings and spread over both sides of ribs.
3. Cover and cook on LOW for 8 hours. (Do NOT remove lid during cooking!)
4. After ribs are finished, move your cooker outside and fire up your handheld smoker. (If you don't have one, then go to step 6!)
5. Place tube from smoker directly in the cooker and cover with the lid. Tape the steam vent shut, if your lid has one. Using hickory chips for the best flavor, add smoke until entire slow cooker is filled. Let the ribs absorb the smoke for 15 minutes then repeat smoking, if desired.
6. Next, baste ribs with your favorite BBQ sauce.
7. If desired, put ribs in an oven-safe dish and place under the broiler for a few minutes to brown and caramelize the BBQ sauce.

FAST
1. Pour apple cider into Crock-Pot® Express. Top with a trivet.
2. Cut rack of pork ribs in half. Mix dry seasonings in a bowl and spread over both sides of ribs.
3. Place both halves side by side on the trivet. Cover with lid and lock into place. Close steam vent. Cook on Meat setting (High pressure) for 20 minutes. Do a Natural Release of the steam for 10 minutes.
4. Follow steps 4-7 of SLOW recipe.

Rump Roast with Au Jus

Roasts made in the slow cooker are always very juicy, and this one is no exception. What's not to love?

YIELD 8 portions **I** **SLOW COOK TIME** 8 to 10 hours **I**
EXPRESS COOK TIME 1 hour 5 minutes

Ingredients

1 T. ground black pepper

1 T. smoked paprika

2 t. chili powder

½ t. celery salt

½ t. ground cayenne pepper

½ t. garlic powder

¼ t. mustard powder

4 lb. rump roast

½ c. water or beef broth

NOTE Add 2 T. oil, 1 c. beef broth and add ½ c. white wine for Crock-Pot® Express.

Directions

SLOW

1. Combine black pepper, paprika, chili powder, celery salt, cayenne pepper, garlic powder and mustard powder in a bowl to make a rub for the meat.
2. Rub the surface of the meat with the combined spices.
3. Transfer roast to your slow cooker, and add water or broth.
4. Cover and cook on LOW for 8 to 10 hours.

FAST

1. Heat oil on Sauté setting.
2. Create a rub by combining pepper, smoked paprika, chili powder, celery salt, cayenne pepper, garlic powder, and mustard powder. Massage the rub into all sides of the meat.
3. Transfer roast to the heated Crock-Pot® Express and sear for 3 minutes on each side. Remove beef and set aside while deglazing the pot.
4. Add wine and broth to the pot. Use a wooden spoon to stir and scrape the bottom of the pot.
5. Turn cooker off and carefully place a trivet inside. Place the roast on the trivet.
6. Cover with lid and close steam vent. Cook on the Beans/Chili setting (Low Pressure) for 5 minutes, then let it stay on the warm setting for 1 hour.
7. Remove the lid and use a meat thermometer to check the internal temperature of the roast (125 degrees F for medium-rare).
8. Remove roast and cover (it will still continue to cook). Let rest for 15 minutes before slicing with a sharp knife. Serve with au jus from the pot.

Cashew Chicken

Make this popular take-out dish in your own home and don't be afraid to put your own spin on it.

YIELD 6 to 8 portions **I** **SLOW COOK TIME** 3 to 4 hours **I**
EXPRESS COOK TIME 5 minutes

Ingredients

- ¼ c. tapioca flour
- ½ t. pepper
- 2 lb. chicken breasts or thighs, cut into 1.5-inch pieces
- Coconut oil
- 1 white onion, chopped
- 3 T. soy sauce or coconut aminos
- 2 T. rice wine vinegar
- 2 T. ketchup
- ½ t. fresh ginger
- ¼ c. diced celery
- ½–1 T. sugar
- 2 garlic cloves, minced
- 2 carrots, peeled and sliced thin
- ½ c. raw cashews
- ¼ t. red pepper flakes (optional)

Directions

SLOW

1. Combine tapioca flour with pepper in a medium bowl.
2. Place the chicken pieces in the flour mixture and toss to coat well.
3. Place the onion and soy sauce in a 4- to 5-quart slow cooker. Add the chicken.
4. Combine the rest of the ingredients in a small bowl and pour over chicken. If desired, sprinkle in red pepper flakes.
5. Cover and cook on LOW for 3 to 4 hours.

FAST

1. Combine tapioca flour with pepper in a medium bowl. Place the chicken pieces in the flour mixture and toss to coat well.
2. Heat coconut oil in the Crock-Pot® Express on Sauté setting. Place the onion, garlic, celery and carrots in the pot and sauté for 3 minutes or until soft.
3. Add the chicken and stir. Drizzle with soy sauce or coconut aminos.
4. Combine remaining ingredients (except cashews) in a small bowl and pour over chicken. Stir well.
5. Cover with lid and close steam vent. Cook on Beans/Chili setting (High Pressure) for 5 minutes.
6. Use a wooden spoon to open steam vent and do a quick release of the pressure. Remove lid and stir in cashews.

For added flavor, toast cashews in a dry, hot skillet until fragrant and mix in!

Ropa Vieja

This traditional Cuban dish makes for the perfect meal on a hot, summer night.

YIELD 8 portions **I** **SLOW COOK TIME** 6 hours **I**
EXPRESS COOK TIME 30 minutes

Ingredients

- 1½ lb. flank steak
- 2 T. coconut oil, divided
- ¼ c. olive oil
- 1 T. white wine vinegar
- 2 T. sea salt
- ¼ c. cilantro, finely chopped
- ¼ c. parsley, finely chopped
- 2 garlic cloves, crushed
- 12 oz. tomato paste, canned
- 1 red bell pepper, thinly sliced
- 1 yellow bell pepper, thinly sliced
- 1 orange bell pepper, thinly sliced
- 1 T. onion flakes (or onion powder)
- 1 T. garlic powder
- 1 T. oregano, dried
- 1 T. cumin powder

NOTE Use 1 lb. of chuck steak and do not slice for the Fast recipe.

Directions

SLOW

1. Cut the flank steak into strips, against the grain.
2. In a frying pan, use 1 T. coconut oil and place in the pan, browning half of the flank steak strips for about 2 to 3 minutes on each side.
3. Repeat with the other half of the flank steak, using the remaining coconut oil.
4. Transfer the browned flank steak to a slow cooker. Add all the remaining ingredients. Mix well, combining all the ingredients with the steak.
5. Cover and cook on LOW for 6 hours.
6. Remove the flank steak and shred. Once shredded, place back in the slow cooker, and again combine all the ingredients with the steak before serving.

FAST

1. Heat oil in Crock-Pot® Express on Sauté setting. Salt and pepper the meat and sear on both sides.
2. Add all the remaining ingredients except the fresh herbs in the pot.
3. Cover with lid and close the steam vent. Cook on Meat setting for 30 minutes. When done, remove the steak and let sit for 10 minutes, then shred.
4. Once shredded, place meat back in the cooker and stir in fresh herbs.

Serve with tortillas, rice, beans or olives!

Meatless
Lentil Tacos

Everybody loves taco night! Switch up your filling with this healthy lentil-laden recipe.

YIELD 6 to 8 portions **I** **SLOW COOK TIME** 9 hours **I**
EXPRESS COOK TIME 25 minutes

Ingredients

- 1 c. chopped onion
- 1 garlic clove, minced
- 1 t. olive oil
- 1 c. dry brown lentils, rinsed
- 1 T. chili powder
- 2 t. ground cumin
- 1 t. oregano
- 1 c. salsa
- 1 (14-oz.) can vegetable broth (beef or chicken broth can be substituted), plus more as needed
- 1 (14-oz.) can corn

TO SERVE (OPTIONAL)

6–8 tortilla shells
- ½ c. grated cheese
- ½ c. sour cream or Greek yogurt
- ¼ c. chopped fresh cilantro
- 1 c. shredded lettuce
  Lime juice, to taste
  Avocado
- ¾ c. chopped fresh tomatoes

NOTE Use 16 oz. broth for Crock-Pot® Express.

Directions

SLOW

1. Combine all ingredients in the slow cooker, except the corn and toppings.
2. Cover and cook on LOW for 9 hours, stirring occasionally and adding broth or water as needed.
3. Stir in corn when done.
4. Fill hard or soft taco shells, top as desired.

FAST

1. Set Crock-Pot® Express to Sauté setting and heat oil. Add chopped onion and garlic. Cook for 2 to 3 minutes.
2. Add remaining ingredients except the corn and toppings. Cover and lock lid. Close steam vent. Cook on Soup setting (High Pressure) for 15 minutes. Do a Natural Release for 10 minutes.
3. Stir in corn and season to taste. Serve in taco shells topped with your favorite ingredients.

Main Meals

Coq au Vin

Savory and delicious, homemade Coq au Vin will make you feel like you're dining at an upscale restaurant in Paris.

YIELD 4 portions **I SLOW COOK TIME** 4 hours 30 minutes to 5 hours 30 minutes **I EXPRESS COOK TIME** 25 minutes

Ingredients

- 1-2 T. canola oil
- 3 lb. chicken thighs and/or legs, skinned
- 1.1 oz. beefy onion soup mix (½ of a 2.2-oz. envelope)
- 1 c. mushrooms, cut into thirds
- ½ onion, coarsely chopped
- 3 carrots, chopped into small pieces
- 1 c. chicken stock
- ½ c. dry red wine
- 1 T. tomato paste
- 1 T. flour
- 2 T. cooked bacon pieces (optional)

Directions

SLOW

1. Heat oil in a skillet on medium-high. Salt and pepper the chicken. Brown chicken, about 5 minutes per side. Place chicken on a paper towel.
2. Add the chicken to a 4- to 5-quart slow cooker and sprinkle with the soup mix.
3. Add mushrooms, onions and carrots. Then pour chicken stock and wine over top.
4. Cover and cook on LOW for 4 to 5 hours.
5. Remove lid and mix tomato paste into sauce; sprinkle with flour and stir. Stir in bacon.
6. Cover and cook for 30 minutes longer.
7. Cut chicken into large pieces and discard bones. Place chicken in bowls and pour stew over top.

FAST

1. Heat oil in the Crock-Pot® Express on the Sauté setting. Salt and pepper the chicken. Brown chicken, cooking about 3 minutes per side.
2. Remove chicken and set on a paper towel. Pour in wine and deglaze the pot.
3. Add chicken back to pot and sprinkle with the soup mix. Add mushrooms, onions and carrots. Pour chicken stock over top.
4. Cover and close steam vent. Cook on Poultry setting (High Pressure) for 15 minutes, followed by 10 minutes Natural Release.
5. Remove lid and mix tomato paste into sauce; sprinkle with flour and stir. Add bacon.
6. Cut chicken into large pieces and discard bones. Place chicken in bowls and pour stew over top.

Carnitas Tacos

You can never go wrong with this flavor-packed shredded pork tacos recipe. Make sure you have some extra tortillas!

YIELD 12 portions **I** **SLOW COOK TIME** 8 to 10 hours **I** **EXPRESS COOK TIME** 35 minutes

Ingredients

1   T. chipotle chili powder
2   t. ground cumin
2   t. garlic powder
1½ t. salt
1   t. onion powder
3   lb. pork loin roast, boneless (can use country style pork ribs too!)
    Tortillas, for serving

NOTE Add 1 c. water for Crock-Pot® Express.

Directions

SLOW

1. Combine all dry ingredients in a small bowl to make the rub.
2. Coat pork with rub and put in the slow cooker.
3. Cover and cook on LOW for 8 to 10 hours or until brown and tender.
4. Remove pork from slow cooker, remove any fat and shred the pork with two forks.
5. Reserve cooking liquid.
6. Stir enough cooking liquid into the pork to moisten.

FAST

1. Heat oil in the Crock-Pot® Express on the Sauté setting. Combine all dry ingredients in a small bowl to make the rub. Coat pork with rub and put in the heated cooker. Brown the pork, about 1 minute per side. Pour in 1 c. water
2. Cover with the lid and close steam vent. Cook on Meat setting (High Pressure) for 35 minutes. Do a Natural Release, then carefully remove lid and test meat temperature.
3. Remove pork from cooker, discard any fat and shred with two forks. Reserve cooking liquid. Stir enough cooking liquid into the pork to moisten.

You can also add avocados, cheese and sour cream for toppings.

Main Meals

Add carrots and potatoes to the cooker for a ready-made side!

Pot Roast

This traditional meal is made easy with this simple slow cooker recipe.

YIELD 6 to 8 portions **I** **SLOW COOK TIME** 6 hours **I**
EXPRESS COOK TIME 1 hour 5 minutes

Ingredients

- 3 lb. beef chuck roast
- 1½ c. water
- 1 dry packet Hidden Valley ranch dressing
- 1 dry packet Italian dressing
- 2 T. soy sauce
  Garlic powder, sprinkle as desired
  Lemon pepper, sprinkle as desired

Directions

SLOW

1. Combine all the ingredients except the garlic powder and lemon pepper for the marinade.
2. Poke roast with knife or fork to make sure marinade gets inside the roast.
3. Sprinkle garlic powder and lemon pepper on bottom of bowl and place roast in the bowl.
4. Pour the mixture over, covering every spot on the roast.
5. Seal the bowl and marinade in the bowl overnight in the refrigerator.
6. Place the roast in a 5- to 6-quart slow cooker, covering again with the marinate.
7. Cover and cook on LOW for 6 hours.

FAST

1. Combine all the ingredients except the garlic powder and lemon pepper for the marinade.
2. Poke roast with knife or fork to make sure marinade gets inside the roast.
3. Sprinkle garlic powder and lemon pepper at bottom of bowl; and place roast in the bowl. Pour the marinade over, covering every spot on the roast. Seal the bowl and marinate overnight in the refrigerator.
4. The next day place the roast and marinade in a Crock-Pot Express®. Cover and close steam vent. Cook on Meat setting for 55 minutes (High Pressure). Do a Natural Release for 10 minutes, then shred with two forks.

Spicy
Chicken Creole Stew

Stress-free dinners, like this delectable dish, always taste better.

YIELD 4 portions I **SLOW COOK TIME** 5 to 12 hours I **EXPRESS COOK TIME** 20 minutes

Ingredients

- 4 boneless skinless chicken breasts, halved
  Salt and pepper, to taste
  Creole-style seasoning, to taste
- 1 (14½-oz.) can stewed tomatoes, with liquid
- 1 stalk celery, diced
- 1 green bell pepper, diced
- 3 garlic cloves, minced
- 1 onion, diced
- 1 (4-oz.) can mushrooms, drained
- 1 jalapeño pepper, seeded and chopped
- 2 c. chicken broth

To make this dish more of a soup, add extra chicken broth.

Directions

SLOW

1. Put chicken in the bottom of a 5-quart slow cooker.
2. Add salt, pepper and Creole-style seasoning, to taste.
3. Add tomatoes, celery, bell pepper, garlic, onion, mushrooms, jalapeño pepper and chicken broth.
4. Cover and cook on LOW for 10 to 12 hours, or on HIGH for 5 to 6 hours.

FAST

1. Season chicken with salt, pepper and creole seasoning. Heat oil on Sauté setting of Crock-Pot® Express.
2. Add onions, garlic, celery and peppers. Cook for 3-4 minutes or until vegetables are softened.
3. Place chicken over vegetables and pour remaining ingredients on top.
4. Cover with lid and close steam vent. Cook on Soup setting (High Pressure) for 10 minutes followed by a 10-minute Natural Release. Serve over rice.

Main Meals

Lumberjack Casserole

After this meal, you'll feel like you're ready to chop down some trees tomorrow.

YIELD 6 to 8 portions I **SLOW COOK TIME** 4 to 8 hours I
EXPRESS COOK TIME 37 minutes

Ingredients

- 1   lb. ground beef
- 1   (15½-oz.) can diced tomatoes
- 1   large onion, diced
- 5   medium potatoes, cubed
- 1   minced fresh garlic clove, or 1½ t. jarred minced garlic
- 1   (16-oz.) can kidney beans
- 1   (10¾-oz.) can cream of mushroom soup
- ½   t. oregano
- ¼   t. freshly ground black pepper
- 1   t. kosher salt
- 2   t. cumin
- 1½ c. grated Pepper Jack

Directions

SLOW

1. In a skillet, brown the ground beef and drain the fat, transferring beef to a slow cooker.
2. Combine all the ingredients except the cheese and stir to mix well.
3. Cover and cook on LOW for 8 hours, or on HIGH for 4 hours.
4. Sprinkle the top with cheese and let cook until melted.

FAST

1. Heat the Crock-Pot® Express on the Sauté setting. Once hot, add ground beef. Salt and pepper the beef, cook and crumble.
2. Drain the fat and add beef back to cooker.
3. Add the rest of the ingredients except the cheese and stir to mix well.
4. Cover and close steam vent. Cook on Soup setting for 12 minutes followed by a 10-minute Natural Release. Remove lid and sprinkle the top of the casserole with cheese. Add lid and close steam vent. Allow casserole to cook on WARM setting for 15 minutes before serving.

If you want a ⋯⋯
heartier meal,
add potatoes
along with the
other veggies!

Island Oxtail

With just a bite of this dish, you'll be transported to an island paradise—no matter the temperature outside.

YIELD 6 to 8 portions **I** **SLOW COOK TIME** 8 hours **I**
EXPRESS COOK TIME 45 minutes

Ingredients

1	T. coconut oil
2	lb. beef oxtails
	Sea salt and pepper, to taste
2	onions, diced
2	carrots, chopped
1	c. shiitake mushrooms, chopped
1	jalapeño pepper, minced
2	c. beef stock
4	garlic cloves, minced
3	T. tomato paste
1	t. ground allspice
1	t. tamarind paste
4	sprigs of fresh thyme
	Fresh parsley and sage

Directions

SLOW

1. Heat coconut oil in a large skillet over medium-high.
2. Season the oxtails with sea salt and pepper. Brown on all sides, about 3 to 4 minutes each side and place in slow cooker.
3. Add the onions, carrots, mushrooms and jalapeño to same skillet. Cook over medium heat for 4 to 5 minutes, or until the onion is translucent.
4. Deglaze the pan by adding the beef stock to skillet, then garlic, tomato paste, allspice and tamarind, scraping up all of the browned bits in skillet.
5. Remove the pan from the heat and pour this sauce over the oxtails in cooker. Cover and cook on LOW 8 hours.

FAST

1. Trim fat from oxtails. Heat coconut oil in the Crock-Pot® Express on Sauté setting.
2. Season oxtails with sea salt and pepper. Brown on all sides, about 2 to 3 minutes per side. Set aside.
3. Add onions, carrots, mushrooms and jalapeño to the Crock-Pot® Express. Add more oil, if needed. Sauté vegetables until the onion is translucent.
4. Stir in the beef stock, then add oxtails, tomato paste, allspice, tamarind and herbs while scraping up all of the browned bits in the cooker.
5. Cover with lid and seal steam vent. Cook on Meat (High Pressure) setting for 45 minutes followed by a quick release. Turn off cooker and allow meat to rest for 10 minutes before serving.

Chicken Tetrazzini

This creamiest of casseroles will quickly be added to your dinner rotation schedule.

YIELD 8 portions **I** **SLOW COOK TIME** 2 hours 30 minutes to 6 hours **I** **EXPRESS COOK TIME** 15 minutes

Ingredients

- 2   lb. boneless, skinless chicken breasts or thighs, cut into 1-inch pieces
- 6   oz. baby Bella mushrooms, cleaned and chopped
- 1   (16-oz.) jar Alfredo sauce
- ¼   c. chicken broth
- 2   T. dry sherry or white wine (optional)
- ¼   t. ground nutmeg
- ¼   t. dried parsley
- ½   red bell pepper, seeded and chopped
     Salt and pepper, to taste
- 1   pkg. freshly cooked fettuccine
- ⅔   c. grated Parmesan cheese
- 2   green onions, thinly sliced

Directions

SLOW

1. Combine chicken and mushrooms in a 3½- to 4-quart slow cooker.
2. Stir together Alfredo sauce, broth, sherry (if desired), nutmeg, parsley, red pepper, salt and pepper in a separate bowl. Pour over mixture in slow cooker.
3. Cover and cook on LOW for 5 to 6 hours or on HIGH for 2 hours 30 minutes to 3 hours.
4. Stir cheese into chicken mixture, and serve over hot cooked fettuccine.

FAST

1. Combine chicken and mushrooms in the Crock-Pot® Express. Stir together pasta sauce, broth, sherry, nutmeg, parsley, red pepper and pepper in a separate bowl. Pour over mixture in the cooker.
2. Cover with lid and close steam vent. Cook on Soup (High Pressure) setting for 5 minutes, followed by a 10-minute Natural Release.
3. Carefully remove lid and stir in cheese until melted. Serve over hot cooked pasta and top with freshly grated Parmesan cheese.

Add frozen peas in step one for extra vegetables!

Perfect Pork Chops

Once you taste slow-cooker pork chops, you'll never cook them another way again.

YIELD 6 portions **I SLOW COOK TIME** 5 hours **I
EXPRESS COOK TIME** 8 minutes

Ingredients

- 2   T. coconut or olive oil
      Salt and pepper, to taste
- 6   boneless pork chops
- 1   sweet onion, sliced

SAUCE INGREDIENTS

- 1   T. sesame oil
- ¼   c. honey
- 1   t. ground ginger
- ½   c. low sodium soy sauce
- ⅓   c. ketchup
- 2   garlic cloves, crushed
      Salt and pepper, to taste

NOTE Add 1 c. water for Crock-Pot® Express.

Directions

SLOW

1. Heat oil in a large skillet over medium-high.
2. Salt and pepper pork chops and brown on each side. Drain oil off chops.
3. Place the sliced sweet onion on the bottom of a 4- to 5-quart slow cooker.
4. Place browned pork chops on top of onions.
5. Combine sauce ingredients, and pour over chops.
6. Cover and cook on LOW for 5 hours, or until internal temperature of pork has reached 145 degrees F by using a meat thermometer.

FAST

1. Heat oil in the Crock-Pot® Express on the Sauté setting. Salt and pepper pork chops and place in the heated pot. Brown both sides of chops, about 1 minute per side. Set aside.
2. Add the sliced sweet onion to the pot and sauté for a few minutes. Pour in water. Place browned pork chops on top of onions and water.
3. Combine sauce ingredients and pour over chops.
4. Cover with lid and seal steam vent. Cook on the Soup (High Pressure) setting for 8 minutes followed by a Natural Release.
5. Remove chops and use a meat thermometer to check the thickest part of the chops to ensure it has reached 145 degrees F. Let the chops rest a few minutes before serving.

Serve with a side of Broccoli Cheese Casserole (pg. 74).

Penne Pasta with Sausage Eggplant Sauce

Hearty and rich, this combo of eggplant and sausage will be a big hit with guests and family alike!

YIELD 6 portions **I SLOW COOK TIME** 3 hours 30 minutes to 7 hours **I EXPRESS COOK TIME** 4 minutes

Ingredients

- 8   oz. hot Italian sausage
- 1   medium eggplant
- 1   (28-oz.) can tomatoes, Italian-style whole peeled in puree, cut up
- 8   oz. button or fresh cremini mushrooms, sliced
- 1   (6-oz.) can tomato paste
- ½   c. onion, chopped
- 6   garlic cloves, minced
- ½   c. dry red wine
- ½   c. assorted fresh herbs (such as flat-leaf parsley, oregano, basil thyme, and/or herbs of your choice)
- ⅓   c. Italian olives, pitted, sliced
  Salt and pepper, to taste
- 6   c. penne pasta, cooked
- ¼   c. grated Parmesan cheese
- 2   T. pine nuts, toasted (optional)

Directions

SLOW

1. Brown sausage in a skillet over medium-high heat. Drain off fat.
2. Peel eggplant and cut into 1-in. cubes. Combine sausage, eggplant, tomatoes, mushrooms, tomato paste, onion, garlic and wine in slow cooker.
3. Cover and cook on LOW for 7 hours or on HIGH for 3 hours 30 minutes.
4. Stir in herbs and olives. Season with salt and pepper, to taste.
5. Cook pasta as directed on the package. Top with the eggplant sauce and cheese.Sprinkle with pine nuts, if desired.

FAST

1. Heat the Crock-Pot® Express on the Sauté setting. Once hot, add the sausage and sauté, crumbling it as it cooks. Remove to a paper towel to absorb any grease.
2. Peel the eggplant and cut into 1-in. cubes. Add sausage, eggplant, pureed tomatoes, mushrooms, tomato paste, onion, garlic and wine in cooker.
3. Stir in uncooked pasta, most of which should be covered with sauce. If not, add enough water to cover. Cover and close vent. Cook on Soup (High Pressure) setting for 4 minutes, followed by a quick release. When finished, stir in herbs and olives. Season with salt and pepper, to taste.

Moroccan Chicken

Get out of your cooking comfort zone with this delicious dinner recipe.

YIELD 7 to 8 portions **I SLOW COOK TIME** 4 to 8 hours **I**
EXPRESS COOK TIME 10 minutes

Ingredients

- 1   t. extra virgin olive oil
- ¼   t. pepper
- ¼   t. ground coriander
- ½   t. ground cinnamon
- 1   t. cumin
- ½   t. paprika
- 7-8 boneless, skinless chicken thighs
- 1   onion, diced
- 2   garlic cloves, minced
- 1   t. grated fresh ginger
- 1   c. canned chickpeas, rinsed
- ½   c. chicken broth
- ⅓   c. raisins
- ⅓   c. dried apricots, sliced
- ½   t. salt

NOTE Use 4 boneless, skinless chicken pieces (breasts or thighs) so they don't overlap for Crock-Pot® Express.

If you don't have dried apricots, other dried fruit like cherries will work!

Directions

1. Add all ingredients in your slow cooker, and stir to combine.
2. Cover and cook on LOW for 8 hours or on HIGH for 4 hours.

FAST

1. Heat oil in the Crock-Pot® Express on Sauté setting.
2. Combine pepper, coriander, cinnamon, cumin and paprika in a bowl. Rub both sides of the chicken with the seasoning mix.
3. Place chicken in prepared cooker and slightly brown on both sides, about 1 minute per side. Remove chicken and add another T. of oil, if needed.
4. Add onions, garlic and ginger to the pot. Stir and cook until ingredients are softened.
5. Add chickpeas, broth, raisins, apricots and salt. Stir well. Add chicken.
6. Cover with lid and seal steam vent. Cook on Soup setting for 10 minutes followed by a quick release. Serve with couscous or grain of your choice.

Main Meals

Honey Mustard Ham

Simple and flavorful, this recipe will take the stress out of your holiday cooking.

YIELD 14 portions **I** **SLOW COOK TIME** 6 to 8 hours **I**
EXPRESS COOK TIME 20 minutes

Ingredients

- 5 lb. pre-cooked bone-in spiral cut ham
- ⅓ c. apple cider
- ¼ c. brown sugar
- 1 T. honey
- 1 T. Dijon mustard
- ⅛ t. black pepper
- ½ t. cinnamon
- ¾ t. ginger

NOTE Add ½ c. water for Crock-Pot® Express.

Directions

SLOW

1. Place ham in large slow cooker and pour apple cider over top.
2. In a small bowl, combine brown sugar, honey, mustard, pepper, cinnamon and ginger; mix well.
3. Rub mixture all over the ham.
4. Cover and cook on LOW for 6 to 8 hours.

FAST

1. Pour water into the Crock-Pot® Express. Place ham inside, sliced side down. Pour apple cider over top.
2. In a small bowl, combine brown sugar, honey, mustard, pepper, ginger and cinnamon; mix well. Rub mixture all over the ham.
3. Cover with lid and close steam vent. Cook on Beans/Chili setting (High Pressure) for 10 minutes followed by a 10 minute Natural Release.
4. Remove ham and allow it to sit a few minutes before slicing. Drizzle with juice from the pot when serving.

Chili Mac and Cheese

Spice up your mac and cheese with a recipe the kids are guaranteed to love!

YIELD 6 to 8 portions **I** **SLOW COOK TIME** 6 to 8 hours **I**
EXPRESS COOK TIME 10 minutes

Ingredients

½   yellow onion, chopped
1   green bell pepper, chopped
1   lb. ground beef, 85% lean
    Salt and pepper, to taste
2   (14½-oz) cans diced tomatoes
1   (6-oz.) can tomato paste
1   envelope Crock-Pot® Original
    Chili Seasoning Mix, or your
    favorite chili seasoning
1   (15-oz.) can pinto beans
1   (15-oz.) can yellow corn, drained
2   T. tapioca, instant
    Your favorite stove top
    macaroni and cheese, prepared

NOTE Remove tapioca and add 1 T. oil, 1 c. elbow macaroni, uncooked and 1 c. grated cheddar cheese for Crock-Pot® Express.

Directions

SLOW

1. Place onion and green pepper in a large skillet over medium-high heat. Sauté until onions are almost translucent.
2. Add beef to skillet. Add salt and pepper and cook until no longer pink. Drain cooked meat and veggie mixture on a paper towel-lined plate.
3. Place meat and veggie mixture in a 5-quart slow cooker.

   Add tomatoes, tomato paste, chili packet, beans, corn and tapioca to the cooker. Stir well to combine. Cover and cook on LOW for 6 to 8 hours.
4. Stir prepared mac and cheese into the chili mixture in the slow cooker. Turn heat to WARM and serve right from the cooker.

FAST

1. Heat 1 T. oil in the Crock-Pot® Express on Sauté setting. Add onion and green pepper to the cooker. Season with salt and pepper. Sauté until onions are almost translucent.
2. Add beef to skillet. Add more salt and pepper and cook until no longer pink. Drain cooked meat and veggie mixture on a paper towel-lined plate.
3. Place meat and veggie mixture in the Crock-Pot® Express. Add tomatoes, paste, chili packet, beans, corn and uncooked noodles. Spoon ingredients over pasta so it is covered. Don't stir!
4. Cover with lid and close the steam vent. Cook on the Beans/Chili setting (High Pressure) for 5 minutes followed by a 5 minute natural release.
5. Carefully remove lid and stir the cheese into the Chili Mac until melted. Top with cheese to serve.

Braised
Leg of Lamb

Your guests will believe you slaved in the kitchen all day over this refined main course. Keep this recipe your little secret.

YIELD 10 to 12 portions **I** **SLOW COOK TIME** 6 to 8 hours **I**
EXPRESS COOK TIME 1 hour 50 minutes

Ingredients

- ⅓   c. fresh mint, chopped
- 3-4   sprigs fresh rosemary,
         chopped
- 2   t. lemon pepper
- 3   garlic cloves, smashed
- ⅛   c. olive oil
- 8   lb. leg of lamb, bone-in
         Sea salt, to taste
- 1   cup red wine
- 1   red onion, chopped
- 3-4   sprigs thyme

NOTE Add 1 c. chicken broth and use a 4 lb. bone-in leg of lamb for Crock-Pot® Express.

Directions

SLOW

1. Make a marinade for the lamb by combining the mint, rosemary, lemon pepper, garlic and olive oil; rub marinade all over the lamb.
2. Next, season with sea salt to your taste. If possible, cover lamb and refrigerate for a few hours or overnight.
3. Remove lamb from marinade; let come to room temperature.

Meanwhile, heat a heavy-bottomed pan over medium-high. Add a touch of olive oil to hot pan and start to sear lamb. Sear on all sides.
4. Add red wine, red onion and thyme sprigs to slow cooker, then place seared lamb into cooker.
5. Cover and cook on LOW for 6 to 8 hours.

FAST

1. Combine mint, rosemary, lemon pepper, garlic and olive oil; rub all over the lamb. Next, season with sea salt. Cover the lamb and refrigerate for a few hours or overnight.
2. When ready to cook, heat olive oil in the Crock-Pot® Express on the Sauté setting. Sear the lamb, about 4 minutes per side.
3. Add broth, red wine, red onion and thyme sprigs to the pot.
4. Cover and seal steam vent. Cook on Meat setting (High Pressure) for 90 minutes followed by a 20-minute Natural Release. Lamb will be fall-off-the-bone tender!

Baked Ziti

This classic Italian dish is perfect for chilly nights.

YIELD 8 portions **I SLOW COOK TIME** 2 to 3 hours **I**
EXPRESS COOK TIME 5 minutes

Ingredients

- 1 lb. 93% lean ground beef
- 1 medium onion, chopped
- 2 t. Italian seasoning
- ½ t. salt
- 1 (64-oz.) jar spaghetti sauce (any kind)
- 15 oz. ricotta cheese
- 2 c. shredded mozzarella
- 1 egg
- 1 c. grated Parmesan cheese
- 16 oz. uncooked ziti noodles

Directions

SLOW

1. Cook ground beef and onion in a large skillet. Crumble the beef as you cook it until no longer pink.
2. Mix in Italian seasoning, salt, and the sauce and set aside.
3. In a separate bowl, combine 1 c. mozzarella, ricotta and Parmesan cheese with egg.
4. Spray your 6-quart slow cooker with non-stick spray or use a slow cooker liner (trust me!).
5. Layer ingredients: Layer 1: (Note: Step 1 and 2 combined make the sauce mix) Pour in 2½ c. sauce mix and spread evenly.

Layer 2: Sprinkle 2 c. of ziti noodles (uncooked) over the sauce mix. Layer 3: Add half of the cheese mixture—drop in balls then carefully spread over noodles.

6. Layer 4: Pour in 2½ c. sauce mix and spread evenly. Layer 5: Sprinkle the rest of the ziti noodles over the sauce mix. Layer 6: Add the other half of the cheese mixture. Again, drop in balls then carefully spread over noodles. Layer 7: Pour in the remaining sauce mix and be sure to cover all the ingredients.
7. Cover and cook on LOW for 4 hours.
8. About 10 minutes before serving, sprinkle with the remaining mozzarella cheese. Serve after the cheese is melted.

FAST

1. Follow steps 1-3 of the SLOW recipe.
2. Cover and cook on Soup setting (High Pressure) for 5 minutes. Do a quick release and carefully remove the lid.
3. Top with remaining mozzarella cheese. Recover and allow to sit, covered for 10 minutes or until cheese is melted.

Main Meals

Asian
Chicken Lettuce Wraps

These lettuce wraps pack a punch and are perfect for a light dinner.

YIELD 6 to 8 portions **I SLOW COOK TIME** 4 to 6 hours **I**
EXPRESS COOK TIME 15 minutes

Ingredients

2–3 lb. boneless chicken thighs,
  cut in 1½-in. pieces
  Salt and pepper, to taste
1 t. garlic powder
½ red bell pepper, thinly sliced
  (or bell pepper of your choice)
4 T. soy sauce
2 T. almond or peanut butter
1 T. honey
2 T. rice wine vinegar
2 t. olive oil
½ t. red pepper flakes
½ t. pepper
1 T. minced ginger
1 carrot, thinly shredded
  Bibb lettuce, for wraps

NOTE Add 1 T. oil for Crock-Pot® Express. Chicken breasts may be used in place of thighs.

Directions

SLOW
1. Liberally season chicken thigh pieces with salt, pepper and garlic powder. Place in slow cooker.
2. Next, combine all other ingredients except carrot and lettuce in small bowl. Pour over chicken.
3. Cover and cook on LOW for 4 hours or until chicken is tender and cooked through.
4. Garnish with shredded carrots or cabbage, chopped jicama, and/or cilantro. Serve in lettuce pieces to make wraps.

FAST
1. Liberally season chicken thigh pieces with salt, pepper and garlic powder.
2. Heat oil in the Crock-Pot® Express on the Sauté setting. Brown chicken, turning frequently so it doesn't cook too much. Turn off sauté setting.
3. Combine all other ingredients in small bowl. Pour over chicken in the pot. Stir to combine.
4. Cover with lid and seal steam vent. Cook on Soup setting (High Pressure) for 5 minutes followed by 10 minutes Natural Release. Open steam vent to release any remaining pressure. Remove lid and stir.
5. Serve in lettuce leaves and top with shredded carrots or cabbage, chopped jicama and cilantro. Drizzle with soy sauce or sauce from the pot.

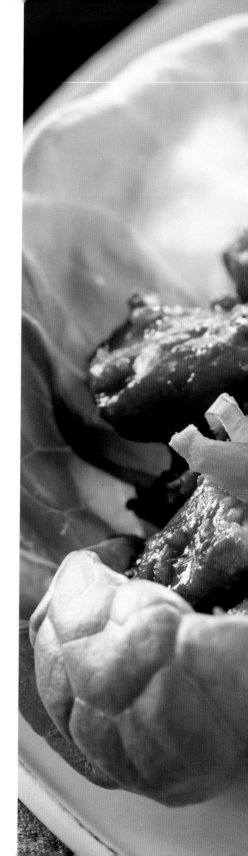

Beer Chicken

Moist and tender, this beer chicken recipe gives you the best of beer-can chicken without the can.

YIELD 8 portions **I SLOW COOK TIME** 6 to 8 hours **I**
EXPRESS COOK TIME 45 minutes

Ingredients

- 1   T. olive oil
- ¼   c. butter, softened
- 1   (1-oz.) package of ranch dressing mix (dry), divided
- 4-5 lb. whole chicken
- 6   slices thick-cut bacon
- 1   c. beer

Directions

SLOW

1. Grease inside of large slow cooker with olive oil.
2. Stir butter and ½ the ranch dressing mix together in a bowl until completely combined.
3. Carefully loosen each side of the skin of the chicken breast and spread the butter-ranch mixture under the skin. Transfer chicken, skin-side up, to slow cooker.
4. Sprinkle remaining ranch dressing mix over chicken. Next, lay bacon strips evenly across bird (I like to weave mine, but any coverage will work). Pour beer around edges of chicken.
5. Cover and cook on LOW for 6 to 8 hours, or until chicken is tender.

FAST

1. Pour beer into to a Crock-Pot® Express. Place trivet inside.
2. Stir butter and half of the ranch mix together in a bowl until completely combined. Carefully loosen each side of the skin covering the chicken breast and spread the butter-ranch mixture under the skin. Transfer chicken to the trivet inside Crock-Pot® Express.
3. Sprinkle remaining half of the ranch dressing mix over chicken. Next, lay bacon strips evenly across bird. Place the chicken on the trivet.
4. Cover with the lid and close the steam vent. Cook on Poultry setting (High Pressure) for 25 minutes, followed by 20 minutes Natural Release.

Shred the chicken after cooking to make it into sandwiches.

Main Meals

Braised Short Ribs

Serve with a side of Cheesy Cauliflower (pg. 89).

Instead of spending a small fortune ordering short ribs off the menu, make these restaurant-quality ribs at home.

YIELD 10 to 12 portions I **SLOW COOK TIME** 8 hours I
EXPRESS COOK TIME 35 minutes

Ingredients

- 2 T. coconut oil or olive oil
   Salt and pepper, to taste
- 4-5 lb. bone-in short ribs
- 2 c. red wine
- 2½ c. beef broth
- 1 (6-oz.) can tomato paste
- 1 T. oregano
- 1 T. rosemary
- 5 garlic cloves, peeled and sliced
- 1 onion, roughly chopped
- 3 celery stalks, chopped
- 2-3 carrots, peeled and chopped
- 3 sweet potatoes, peeled and cut in chunks

NOTE Add 1 T. tapioca for Crock-Pot® Express.

Directions

SLOW

1. Heat skillet over medium-high and add oil. Salt and pepper all sides of meat. Once pan is hot, sear all sides of short ribs. Place browned beef in slow cooker.
2. Add wine and beef broth to skillet to deglaze pan, scraping up any bits on the bottom of pan. Add tomato paste and stir 2 to 3 minutes; add this mixture to the cooker. Add seasonings and all vegetables. Cover and cook on for LOW 8 hours.

FAST

1. Heat the coconut oil in a Crock-Pot® Express on the sauté setting. Salt and pepper the meat and sear all sides of short ribs.
2. Set ribs aside and add celery, onions and carrots. Cook for 3 minutes, stirring every 30 seconds. Pour wine and beef stock in pot and bring to a simmer. Scrape up any bits on bottom of pan. Let sauce simmer for about 10 minutes or until liquid has decreased by half. Stir in tomato paste, meat and remaining seasonings to pot.
3. Cover with the lid and seal steam vent. Cook on Meat setting (High Pressure) for 35 minutes followed by a quick release of steam. Carefully remove ribs and set aside.
4. Turn cooker to Sauté setting. Simmer sauce in pot and stir in a slurry of ¼ c. water and tapioca. Allow to continue simmering until the sauce has thickened. Serve short ribs drizzled with sauce.

Classic
Cajun Jambalaya

One bite of this spicy Louisiana classic, and you'll be transported to the French Quarter.

YIELD 8 portions **I** **SLOW COOK TIME** 3 to 6 hours **I**
EXPRESS COOK TIME 17 minutes

Ingredients

2	lb. boneless, skinless chicken breasts (cut into 1 ½ inch pieces)
½	c. diced green bell pepper
2	c. diced celery
1	c. chopped yellow onions
1	(14.5-oz.) can diced tomatoes
2	c. chicken broth
1	(6-oz.) can tomato paste
2	garlic cloves, minced
3	T. Cajun seasoning
1	t. sea salt
1	lb. raw shrimp, peeled and deveined
2	c. basmati rice
1	bay leaf

Directions

SLOW

1. Combine chicken breasts, bell pepper, celery, onion, tomatoes, chicken broth, tomato paste, garlic, seasoning and salt into large slow cooker.
2. Cover and cook on LOW for 6 hours, or HIGH for 3 hours.
3. Add shrimp to cooker, stirring to combine. Cover and cook on LOW for an additional 2 hours or on HIGH for 1 hour.
4. Cook brown rice according to the directions on the package, stirring in once the shrimp is cooked.

FAST

1. Heat oil on the Sauté setting in a Crock-Pot® Express. Add bell pepper, garlic, celery and onion. Cook for 2 minutes or until onion is soft.
2. Salt and pepper the chicken and add to the pot. Sear chicken, stirring a few times to brown all sides (about 2 minutes total).
3. Turn cooker off and add rice, tomatoes, chicken broth, tomato paste, cajun seasoning and salt.
4. Cover with lid and close steam vent. Cook on (Setting) for 7 minutes, followed by a quick release. 5. Stir shrimp into the pot and recover. Let the pot sit for about 10 minutes for shrimp to cook through.

Turkey and Bean Chili

This recipe is very versatile—use any canned beans you have on hand.

You can make this crowd-pleasing main for a group, or freeze some for lunches or dinner later in the week.

YIELD 8 portions **I SLOW COOK TIME** 8 hours **I**
EXPRESS COOK TIME 15 minutes

Ingredients

- ½ onion, diced
- 2 carrots, chopped
- 2 stalks celery, chopped
- 1 lb. ground turkey breast
- 1 can kidney beans (do not drain)
- 1 (14-oz.) can diced tomatoes
- 1.5 c. beef broth
- 1 (6-oz.) can tomato paste
- 1 (4-oz.) can diced green chilies
- 1.5 T. chili powder
- 1 t. cumin
- 1 T. minced garlic
- 1 bay leaf

Directions

SLOW

1. Place onion, carrot and celery in the bottom of a 6-quart slow cooker.
2. Add raw ground turkey, in chunks, then add remaining ingredients.
3. Cover and cook on LOW for 8 hours, stirring and breaking up meat after 4 hours.
4. Remove bay leaf before serving.

FAST

1. Heat oil on the Sauté setting in the Crock-Pot® Express. Place onion, carrot, celery and ground turkey in the pot. Season with salt and pepper.
2. Sauté for about 3 minutes, crumbling turkey as it cooks. It's OK if turkey isn't cooked through. Add remaining ingredients.
3. Cover with lid and seal steam vent. Cook on the Soup setting (High Pressure) for 5 minutes, followed by a 10-minute Natural Release. Remove bay leaf before serving.

Balsamic Pork Tenderloin

This tenderloin makes for the perfect autumn dinner.

YIELD 12 portions **I SLOW COOK TIME** 8 to 9 hours **I**
EXPRESS COOK TIME 18 minutes

Ingredients

- 2 small pork tenderloins
  Salt and pepper, to taste
- 4 apples, peeled and sliced
- 1 small onion, chopped
- 1 t. minced garlic
- 1 t. dried rosemary
- 1 T. olive oil
- ¼ c. balsamic glaze
- ¾ c. apple juice

Directions

SLOW

1. Heat oil in a pan over medium-high.
2. Salt and pepper pork. Once the oil is hot, add the pork and sear on each side; about 3 minutes.
3. Place onions, garlic and apples over the pork in slow cooker.
4. In a small bowl, combine rosemary, balsamic glaze and juice. Pour over ingredients in cooker. Cover and cook on LOW for 90 minutes.
5. Test internal temperature of pork with a meat thermometer.
6. Set pork aside to rest before cutting. Top with apples and sauce from multi-cooker when serving.

FAST

1. Use the Sauté setting and heat oil in the Crock-Pot® Express.
2. Salt and pepper pork. Once the oil is hot, add the pork and sear on each side; about 3 minutes.
3. Remove tenderloins and add onions and garlic. Sauté until onions are tender. Then add apples.
4. In a small bowl, combine rosemary, balsamic glaze and juice. Pour into cooker.
5. Add pork to the pot. Cover and lock lid into place. Select Steam setting (Low Pressure) for 3 minutes.
6. Turn the power off and allow the pressure to Natural Release for 15 minutes. Test internal temperature of pork with a meat thermometer.
7. Set pork aside to rest before cutting. Top with apples and sauce from cooker when serving.

Main Meals

Bali's
Beef & Broccoli

Skip the takeout and just make this meaty main yourself! You won't notice the difference.

YIELD 6 portions **I SLOW COOK TIME** 4 hours **I**
EXPRESS COOK TIME 20 minutes

Ingredients

- 1½ lb. chuck roast, cut into 1½-in. pieces
- 1 T. minced garlic
- 1 medium yellow onion
- ¼ c. soy sauce
- ¾ c. beef broth
- ¼ cup brown sugar
- ⅓ c. sesame oil, divided
- ¼ c. oyster sauce
- 1 T. cornstarch, plus 3 T. water, mixed
- 16 oz. frozen broccoli
  Rice, for serving

Directions

SLOW

1. Add meat and all ingredients except cornstarch, water and broccoli to the cooker. Stir well and lock lid in place.
2. Cook on HIGH for 3 hours 30 minutes. Carefully remove lid and stir in cornstarch/water and broccoli. Cover and slow cook for 30 more minutes, or until broccoli is just tender.
3. Stir and serve immediately over hot rice.

FAST

1. Set Crock-Pot® Express to sauté setting and add oil. Add meat and sear until browned, about 2 minutes. Next add garlic and onions. Sauté about 2 more minutes.
2. In a small bowl, combine soy sauce, broth and sugar. Pour over meat in pot. Add lid to pot and lock in place. Ensure steam vent is sealed.
3. Cook on Manual/High setting for 10 minutes.
4. Once finished, allow steam to release naturally for 5 minutes. Carefully open steam vent and move lid.
5. Stir in cornstarch and then add broccoli. Lock lid back in place and cook on Manual/High for one more minute.
6. Once finished, allow steam to release naturally for 5 minutes. Stir and serve immediately over hot rice.

This bread-pudding will basically melt in your mouth.

Dessert

We all know dessert is the best part of every meal, so you better save room for all of these sugary-sweet recipes.

Strawberries and Cream Bread Pudding

Fluffy, sweet and sugary, you'll want to eat this dessert for breakfast.

YIELD 12 portions **I SLOW COOK TIME** 4 to 5 hours **I EXPRESS COOK TIME** 15 minutes

Ingredients

- 1 (21½-in.) loaf French bread (stale is OK!)
- 8 strawberries, washed and thinly sliced
- 2 c. whole milk
- 4 T. strawberry jam
- 1 t. vanilla
- 1 t. cinnamon
- ⅛ t. nutmeg
- 4 eggs
- ½ c. sugar
- 3 oz. cream cheese, cubed (optional)

Directions

SLOW

1. Grease a slow cooker with nonstick cooking spray.
2. Tear bread into 2-in. pieces and place in the slow cooker.
3. Slice strawberries into small pieces and scatter over the bread. If desired, sprinkle cubed cream cheese over strawberry layer.
4. In a blender, combine all remaining ingredients. Pour liquid ingredients over bread and strawberries in the slow cooker. Push down a bit on the bread to make sure it's completely covered with the liquid.
5. Cover and cook on LOW for 4 to 5 hours.
6. Remove lid and switch cooker to the "off" position. Use potholders to remove the insert set on a hot pad. Allow to cool for 10 minutes before serving.
7. To serve, dish into small bowls and top with ice cream OR top with butter and a light sprinkle of powdered sugar.

FAST

1. Grease a round cake pan or other dish that fits inside the Crock-Pot® Express. Pour ½ c. water into the Crock-Pot® Express. Place trivet in cooker.
2. Tear bread into 2-in. pieces and place in the dish. Slice strawberries into small pieces and scatter over the bread.
3. If desired, sprinkle cubed cream cheese over strawberry layer. (This is how my daughter likes it!)
4. In a blender, combine all remaining ingredients. Pour liquid ingredients over bread and strawberries in the cake pan/dish. Push down a bit on the bread to make sure it's completely covered with the liquid. Cover with a paper towel and then a piece of foil. Carefully place pan on top of trivet inside the Crock-Pot® Express.
5. Place lid on top and seal steam vent. Cook on Dessert setting (High Pressure) for 15 minutes followed by a quick release. Remove lid and switch cooker to the "off" position.
6. Use potholders to remove the insert from the pot and set on a hot pad. Allow to cool for 10 minutes before serving.
7. To serve, dish into small bowls and top with ice cream or top with butter and a light sprinkle of powdered sugar.

This recipe is a great way to get rid of stale bread or leftover French toast!

Desserts

Dessert Apples

Put a twist on your preferred healthy snack and turn it into your new favorite dessert.

YIELD 4 portions **I SLOW COOK TIME** 2 to 3 hours **I**
EXPRESS COOK TIME 13 minutes

Ingredients

- ½ c. butter, melted
- ¼ c. nut butter (such as peanut or almond)
- 2 T. cinnamon
- ⅛ t. nutmeg
- ⅛ t. salt
- 4 apples of your choice, cored
- 1 c. water
- 4 T. shredded unsweetened coconut, plus more for topping
- ½ c. dried apricots, figs or dates (optional)

Directions

SLOW

1. Mix butters; add cinnamon, nutmeg and salt to butter mixture.
2. Place apples in slow cooker and add water to bottom.
3. Spoon coconut and almond butter mixture into each apple until full. Add dried fruit at this point, if desired.
4. Sprinkle a bit more cinnamon to tops of apples and then add shredded coconut.
5. Cover and cook on LOW for 2 to 3 hours, until apples reach desired softness.

FAST

1. Core apples and set aside. Mix coconut butter and almond butters; add cinnamon, nutmeg and salt to butters.
2. Add ½ c. water to the Crock-Pot® Express. Place apples in the cooker. Spoon coconut and almond butter mixture into each apple until full. Add dried fruit at this point, if desired. Sprinkle a bit more cinnamon to tops of apples and then add additional shredded coconut.
3. Cover and lock lid into sealing position. Cook on Dessert (Low Pressure) setting for 3 minutes followed by a Natural Release for 10 minutes.

Pick up apples from your local farmer's market, so they're extra fresh.

Tapioca Pudding

Comforting and simple, this pudding is the perfect treat after a rich dinner.

YIELD 8 portions **I SLOW COOK TIME** 3 to 6 hours **I**
EXPRESS COOK TIME 18 minutes

Ingredients

- 2 eggs, lightly beaten
- 4 c. milk
- ⅔ c. white sugar
- 2 t. vanilla
- ½ c. small pearl tapioca (not instant)

Sprinkle cinnamon over top if desired!

Directions

SLOW

1. Mix eggs, milk, sugar, vanilla, and tapioca. Add to slow cooker.
2. Cover and cook on HIGH for 3 hours or on LOW for 6 hours.
3. Make sure to stir often while cooking.

FAST

1. Pour 1 c. water in the Crock-Pot® Express insert and place a trivet inside.
2. In a medium bowl, mix eggs, milk, sugar, vanilla and tapioca. Pour in an ovenproof dish that fits inside the Crock-Pot® Express. Place dish on trivet and close the lid. Seal steam vent. Cook on Multigrain setting (High Pressure) for 13 minutes followed by a 5 minute Natural Release.
3. Carefully remove dish and stir the tapioca well. Spoon into individual serving dishes, cover with plastic wrap and refrigerate a few hours before serving.

Desserts

Mexican Flan

This classic Mexican dessert is so velvety you'll want seconds.

YIELD 6 portions **I SLOW COOK TIME** 3 hours 30 minutes to 4 hours **I EXPRESS COOK TIME** 19 minutes

Ingredients

1½ c. sugar, divided

1   t. lemon juice

6   large eggs

1   (14-oz.) can sweetened
    condensed milk

3¼ c. milk

1   t. vanilla

Directions

SLOW

1. Warm a pan over medium heat and pour in 1 c. sugar.

2. Constantly stir sugar until it browns and becomes caramelized. Once desired color is reached, pour lemon juice over the sugar to stop it from browning.

3. Quickly pour caramel into ramekins that will fit in slow cooker. Tilt to swirl the caramel around the sides of the ramekins.

4. Whisk eggs in a bowl. Add in milk, then slowly mix in ½ c. sugar and vanilla. (Blend well after each ingredient is added.)

5. Pour custard into the ramekins (over the caramel).

6. Cover and cook on HIGH for 3 hours 30 minutes to 4 hours.

7. Insert a knife just to the side of the center. If knife comes out clean, the flan is ready.

Remove and let cool for a few minutes then refrigerate for at least 1 hour.

9. Using a knife, cut around the edges of each ramekin and turn upside down on a plate (to remove custard.)

10. Spoon any additional caramel sauce from ramekin over the custard and serve.

FAST

1. Heat Crock-Pot® Express on Sauté setting. Add 1 c. of sugar with 2 T. water and stir constantly until it browns and becomes caramelized. Once desired color is reached, pour lemon juice over the sugar to stop it from browning.

2. Quickly pour caramel into prepared ramekins that will fit on a trivet in cooker.

3. Make custard mix: Whisk eggs in a bowl then add milk followed by ½ c. sugar. Blend in vanilla.

4. Pour custard mixture into the ramekins (over top caramel) and cover each one tightly with foil.

5. Carefully clean out the cooking insert and place back into the Crock-Pot® Express. Pour ½ c. water into the cooker.

6. Place a trivet inside and put the ramekins on the trivet.

7. Cover with lid and close steam vent. Cook on Soup setting (High Pressure) for 9 minutes followed by a 10 minute Natural Release. Transfer to refrigerator to cool for a few hours.

8. Using a knife, cut around the edges of each ramekin and turn upside down on a plate (to remove custard). Spoon any additional caramel sauce from ramekin over custard and serve.

Turn It!

If you find that one side of your slow cooker gets hotter than the other, try turning the insert halfway through cooking time. If you're not sure, do it just in case—especially for recipes with cream-based sauces, which will be more likely to burn.

Bananas Foster Bread Pudding

Wow family and friends alike with this complex and stunningly sweet pudding.

YIELD 6 to 8 portions **I SLOW COOK TIME** 2 hours **I EXPRESS COOK TIME** 15 minutes

Ingredients

- 2 c. bread cubes
- 4 bananas, peeled and sliced
- 2 eggs, beaten
- 1 c. heavy cream or half-and-half
- 4 T butter, melted
- 1 c. packed brown sugar
- ⅛–¼ c. spiced rum
- 1 t. vanilla extract
- 1 t. ground cinnamon
- ¼ c. chopped pecans or walnuts
- ¼ c. shredded coconut (optional)

Directions

SLOW

1. Grease inside of slow cooker with oil. Layer bread cubes on bottom of cooker. Next, layer sliced bananas on top of bread.
2. Combine eggs, cream, butter, brown sugar, rum, vanilla and cinnamon in a small bowl; pour over bananas and bread.
3. Cover and cook on LOW for 1 hour 30 minutes hours, twisting the insert half way around after about 1 hour.
4. Sprinkle nuts and coconut over top and cook an additional 30 minutes.

FAST

1. Grease the inside of a cake pan or other ovenproof dish that will fit inside the Crock-Pot® Express. Place bread cubes then banana slices in the dish.
2. Combine eggs, cream, butter, brown sugar, rum, vanilla and cinnamon in a small bowl; pour over bananas and bread. Sprinkle with nuts and coconut.
3. Cover with a paper towel and then tightly with foil. Pour ½ c. water into the cooking pot and place a trivet inside. Put the foil covered dish on the trivet.
4. Cook on Dessert setting (High Pressure) for 15 minutes followed by a quick release. Remove lid and switch cooker to the "off" position.
5. Use potholders to remove the insert from the pot and set on a hot pad. Allow to cool for 10 minutes before serving.

Desserts

Cinnamon Fudge

Impress your guests with this scrumptious and unique type of fudge, which will have them begging for the recipe.

YIELD 20 portions **I** **SLOW COOK TIME** 6 hours **I**
EXPRESS COOK TIME 3 hours

Ingredients

2½ c. good quality dark chocolate
    chips, like Ghirardelli

¼ c. coconut milk, canned

¼ c. honey

    Dash of sea salt

1 t. pure vanilla extract

1 t. cinnamon

Directions

SLOW

1. Generously grease a 2-quart slow cooker with nonstick spray.
2. Add chocolate, coconut milk, honey and a dash of sea salt to cooker; stir to combine.
3. Cover and cook on LOW for 2 hours without stirring. Do not lift the lid during cooking!
4. Turn cooker off and remove lid. Add vanilla and cinnamon, stirring to combine. Cool in uncovered cooker until fudge has reached room temp (about 3 to 4 hours).
5. After 4 hours, stir fudge for several minutes until the sheen that was on top is all gone. Pour the fudge into a greased 1-quart glass dish.

Cover and refrigerate 4 hours or until firm.

FAST

1. Heat the Crock-Pot® Express on the Low Sauté setting.
2. Add all ingredients and stir to combine while they are melting. Note: Don't let the chocolate scorch. If pot appears to be too hot, switch from Sauté to Warm setting.
3. Meanwhile, line a baking sheet with foil. Generously grease the baking sheet with coconut oil.
4. Continue stirring fudge mixture in the pan until all ingredients are melted.
5. Pour fudge into the foiled pan. Refrigerate and allow to firm; about 3 hours.
6. Cut into squares, then refrigerate and allow to firm again.

Indulge a little with a high-quality dark chocolate!

Vanilla Applesauce

When the leaves begin to fall, swap out your usual applesauce recipe with our sweet take.

YIELD 6 to 8 portions **I SLOW COOK TIME** 3 to 4 hours **I EXPRESS COOK TIME** 20 minutes

Ingredients

- 2 lbs. Honey Crisp apples, peeled and cored (or your favorite apple)
- ½ c. apple cider
- 2 T. lemon juice
- 2 t. vanilla extract
- 1½ t. cinnamon
- ½ t. nutmeg

Directions

SLOW

1. Place apples in bottom of slow cooker. Then, add the rest of the ingredients to the cooker and stir to combine with apples.
2. Cover and cook on LOW for 3 to 4 hours or until apples are easily mashed.
3. Mash apple mixture with a potato masher, or if you prefer no chunks, use a hand-held blender to purée.
4. Applesauce will stay good for up to one week in the refrigerator. You can also freeze in individual portions and use as needed.

FAST

1. Peel, core, and slice apples. Place in bottom of the Crock-Pot Express®. Add the rest of the ingredients and stir to combine with apples.
2. Cover with lid and close steam vent. Cook on Soup (High Pressure) setting for 5 minutes followed by a 15-minute Natural Release.
3. Mash apple mixture with a potato masher right in the pot. If you prefer no chunks, use a hand-held blender to purée.
4. Applesauce will stay good for up to one week in the refrigerator. You can also freeze in individual portions and use as needed.

S'mores Brownies

Level up your campfire s'mores with this scrumptious and rich brownie recipe.

YIELD 16 portions **I** **SLOW COOK TIME** 1 hour 30 minutes to 2 hours **I** **EXPRESS COOK TIME** 25 minutes

Ingredients

- 2⅓ c. milk chocolate chips, divided
- 10 T. unsalted butter
- 2 large eggs
- 2 t. vanilla
- 1 c. extra fine sugar
- 2 T. unsweetened cocoa powder
- ¼ t. salt
- ¾ c. all-purpose flour
- 16 individual graham crackers
- 3 c. mini marshmallows

Directions

SLOW

1. Line your slow cooker with aluminum foil and spray the foil with nonstick spray.
2. Microwave ¼ c. chocolate chips with butter at 50 percent power in 15 second increments. Stir after each time until smooth.
3. In a separate bowl, beat eggs and vanilla with sugar. Slowly add in the melted chocolate/butter mixture until well combined.
4. In a small bowl, sift together cocoa, salt and flour. Add mixture to rest of batter. Do not overmix.
5. Pour half of the batter into your prepared cooker. Top with whole graham crackers, breaking and piecing together at edges as needed to fully cover brownie batter.
6. Sprinkle remaining chocolate chips on top of graham crackers and then top with the remaining brownie batter.
7. Cover and cook on LOW for 1 hour 30 minutes to 2 hours.
8. Check the brownies for doneness. They will look undercooked on top but pull a bit on the foil to really check doneness. If the brownies lift easily without buckling, remove from slow cooker and allow to cool. If they buckle, allow to bake for 15 more minutes, checking again, until ready to remove.
9. Once cooled, top with marshmallows and place under oven broiler for 30 to 60 seconds, until marshmallows are toasted. (Watch closely as marshmallows can quickly burn.) Once tops are toasted remove brownies from oven, cut and serve.

FAST

1. Heat Crock-Pot® Express on Low Sauté setting. Add ¼ c. chocolate chips and the butter, stirring every 15 seconds until melted and smooth.
2. Beat eggs and vanilla with sugar in a medium mixing bowl. Slowly pour the melted chocolate/butter mixture into the mixing bowl. Stir until well combined.
3. In a small bowl, sift together cocoa, salt and flour. Slowly add mixture to the chocolate batter while stirring. Do not overmix.
4. Grease a 7-in. springform pan and pour half the batter into the pan. Top with whole graham crackers, breaking and piecing together at edges as needed to fully cover brownie batter. Sprinkle remaining chocolate chips on top of graham crackers and then top with the remaining brownie batter. Cover with paper towel and then tightly with foil.
5. Pour ½ c. water into cooker and place trivet inside. Lock lid and close steam vent. Cook on Multigrain setting for 25 minutes followed by a quick release of steam. Turn off cooker and carefully remove pan. Remove foil and allow brownies to cool.
6. Top with marshmallows and place under the broiler or for 30 to 60 seconds, until marshmallows are toasted. (Watch closely as marshmallows can quickly burn.)
7. Once tops are toasted remove brownies from oven, cut and serve.

Coconut Rice Pudding

This tasty Thai treat will prove there's more to dessert than chocolate.

YIELD 6 portions **I SLOW COOK TIME** 4 to 5 hours **I**
EXPRESS COOK TIME 20 minutes

Ingredients

- 2¾ c. water
- ¾ c. long-grain white rice
- 1 (15-oz.) can cream of coconut
- 1 (12-oz.) can evaporated milk
- 1 t. vanilla
- ⅔ c. sweetened coconut flakes (optional)
- 1 T. dark rum (optional)

Directions

SLOW

1. Stir water, rice, cream of coconut and evaporated milk until combined, and pour in a slow cooker. Cover and cook on LOW for 4 hours.
2. Turn off slow cooker and remove lid. Stir in rum, if desired. Let pudding stand 10 minutes, then stir again.
3. Transfer pudding to serving bowls and refrigerate for 1 hour before serving.

FAST

1. Place water, rice, cream of coconut and evaporated milk in the Crock-Pot® Express and stir well to dissolve sugar.
2. Cover with lid and close steam vent. Cook on Multigrain setting for 20 minutes. Carefully do a quick release of the steam. Stir in rum, if desired.
3. Let pudding stand 10 minutes. Transfer pudding to serving bowls and refrigerate for 1 hour before serving.

Add any fruit you'd like to this Coconut Rice Pudding.

Apple Bread

This sweet and easy dessert will be a family favorite after the first bite.

YIELD 6 portions I **SLOW COOK TIME** 4 hours I
EXPRESS COOK TIME 1 hour 10 minutes

Ingredients

½   c. whole milk
1   egg
1½ c. flour
1   T. baking powder
½   t. salt
1   T. butter, melted
1   c. apple pie filling
1   T. cinnamon
1   T. brown sugar

Directions

SLOW

1. Gently whisk the milk and
   egg in a medium bowl.
   Fold in flour, baking powder, salt
   and butter.
2. Once combined, spoon in the
   apple pie filling and cinnamon.
   Stir gently.
3. Spray a slow cooker generously
   with nonstick spray.
4. Pour batter into the slow cooker
   and smooth to ensure it is even.
   Sprinkle brown sugar over top.
5. Cover and cook on HIGH for 4
   hour or until a toothpick comes
   out clean.

FAST

1. Gently whisk the milk, egg and
   butter in a medium bowl.
2. In a small bowl combine the
   flour, baking powder and salt.
   Fold dry mixture into the wet
   ingredients. Stir until just
   combined. Spoon in the apple
   pie filling and cinnamon. Stir
   gently.
3. Spray a 7-in. springform pan
   generously with non-stick spray.
4. Pour batter into the prepared
   pan and sprinkle brown sugar
   over top. Cover pan with a large
   paper towel and then tightly
   with foil.
5. Pour ½ c. water into the Crock-
   Pot® Express and set trivet
   inside. Place springform pan on
   top of trivet.
6. Cover cooker with lid and
   close the steam vent. Cook
   on Multigrain setting for
   60 minutes followed by a
   10 minute natural release.
   Carefully remove lid and lift
   pan out of cooker.
7. Remove foil and paper towel
   and allow bread to cool before
   serving.

Chocolate
Upside Down Cake

Turn your dessert menu upside down with this chocolately cake.

YIELD 6 to 8 portions **I** **SLOW COOK TIME** 2 hours 30 minutes **I** **EXPRESS COOK TIME** 8 minutes

Ingredients

- 1 c. flour
- 1.5 t. baking powder
- ¼ t. salt
- 1 T. butter, melted
- 1 c. sugar, divided
- ⅓ c. plus 3 T. unsweetened cocoa
- ½ c. milk
- 1 t. vanilla
- 1⅔ c. hot water

Directions

SLOW

1. Mix flour, baking powder, salt, butter, ½ c. sugar, 3 T. cocoa, milk and vanilla.
2. Spoon batter evenly into lightly greased slow cooker.
3. Mix remaining sugar, cocoa and hot water. Pour over the batter in the slow cooker. Do not stir!
4. Cover and cook on HIGH for 2 hours 30 minutes or until center of cake springs back to touch.

FAST

1. Prepare 4 ramekins by spraying generously with non-stick cooking spray.
2. Mix flour, baking powder, salt, ½ c. sugar, 3 T. cocoa, milk, melted butter and vanilla. Spoon batter evenly into ramekins.
3. Mix remaining sugar, cocoa, and hot tap water in a glass measuring cup. Evenly pour the sugar mixture over the batter in each ramekin. Do not stir!
4. Pour 1 c. water in the bottom of the Crock-Pot® Express and place a trivet inside. Place three ramekins on the trivet and stack the fourth on top.
5. Cover with lid and seal steam vent. Cook on Multigrain setting for 8 minutes followed by a quick release. Carefully take off the lid and remove ramekins.
6. Invert each ramekin onto a plate and serve immediately with ice cream or topped with whipped cream.

You can also sprinkle with powdered sugar, if desired.

Crème Brûlée

There's no better feeling than cracking the brittle surface of this sugary sweet dessert.

YIELD 4 portions I **SLOW COOK TIME** 2 to 4 hours I
EXPRESS COOK TIME 23 minutes

Ingredients

5	egg yolks
2	c. heavy cream
½	c. fine sugar
1	T. vanilla extract
¼	c. raw sugar, to garnish

Directions

SLOW

1. Use a heat-resistant dish that fits inside slow cooker and place it inside. Using a cup or pitcher, pour water around the edges so there is water ½ to ¾ of the way up the sides of the dish. Push it down with your hand if it starts to float up. Take the dish back out. If you have separate dessert ramekins, do the same thing after nestling them all inside.
2. Whip the egg yolks in a bowl and slowly add the cream and fine sugar while mixing.
3. Add the vanilla. Pour mixture into the dish and carefully lower into the cooker without sloshing water into the dish.
4. Cover and cook on HIGH for 2 to 4 hours.
5. Very carefully remove dish and let cool completely on counter, then chill in the refrigerator for 2 to 3 hours.

6. Sprinkle the raw sugar evenly over the top of the custard. Move your oven rack to the top rack and broil for 3 to 10 minutes, checking often for sugar to caramelize. Cool again in the fridge for a few hours.

FAST

1. Pour 1 c. water into the Crock-Pot® Express. Place trivet inside the pot.
2. Whip the egg yolks in a bowl and slowly add the cream, sugar and vanilla. Pour mixture into an ovenproof dish that fits inside the cooking insert. Place a paper towel on top of the dish and then cover tightly with foil. Carefully place dish on the trivet.
3. Cover with lid and close steam vent. Cook on High Pressure for 8 minutes followed by a 15-minute Natural Release. Remove lid and carefully remove the ramekins.
4. Place dish in the refrigerator to cool for two hours before serving. If desired, just before serving, sprinkle raw sugar on top and caramelize with a handheld torch.

Top with
strawberries and
strawberry sauce.

Creamy
Cheesecake

After taking a bite of this cheesecake, you'll feel like you've found your own little slice of heaven.

YIELD 6 portions I **SLOW COOK TIME** 3 hours I
EXPRESS COOK TIME 53 minutes

Ingredients

1	c. graham cracker crumbs
¼	c. brown sugar
¼	c. butter, melted
2	large eggs
16	oz. cream cheese, softened
¾	c. sugar
¼	c. heavy cream
1	t. vanilla
1	T. flour

Directions

SLOW

1. Combine graham cracker crumbs, brown sugar and butter and press into springform pan that will fit inside slow cooker.
2. In a bowl, beat eggs well. Add cheese and sugar and continue to blend until fluffy. Add cream, vanilla and flour and beat an additional 2 minutes. Pour mixture on top of crust.
3. Line cooker with crumpled foil. Insert springform pan.
4. Cover and cook on HIGH for 3 hours.
5. Turn off heat and leave cheesecake in slow cooker for another hour or until cool enough to remove.
6. Move to rack to cool completely. Chill for 1 hour before serving.

FAST

1. Combine graham cracker crumbs, brown sugar and butter and press into a 7-in. springform pan lined with parchment paper.
2. Beat eggs well, then add cheese and sugar. Continue to blend until fluffy. Add cream, vanilla and flour and beat an additional 2 minutes. Pour mixture on top of crust.
3. Cover springform pan with paper towel and then cover in foil.
4. Place a trivet inside the Crock-Pot® Express and pour 1 c. water inside. Put the spring form pan on top of the trivet.
5. Cover with the lid and close the steam vent. Cook on Multigrain setting (High Pressure) for 35 minutes followed by an 18 minute Natural Release.
6. Remove pan and check for doneness. Cake should be firm but inside should have just a bit of movement.
7. Place cheesecake in the refrigerator overnight to chill before serving.

Banana Bread

This is a great way to use ripe or browning bananas.

Although the recipe is in the dessert section, you can snack on this banana bread all day long.

YIELD 8 portions **I SLOW COOK TIME** 2 to 3 hours **I**
EXPRESS COOK TIME 50 minutes

Ingredients

- ⅓ c. unsalted butter
- ½ c. sugar
- 2 eggs, at room temperature
- 1¾ c. flour
- 1 tsp. baking powder
- ½ tsp. salt
- ½ tsp. baking soda
- 3 ripe bananas, mashed
- ½ c. chocolate chips (optional)
- ½ c. raisins (optional)
- ½ c. walnuts (optional)

Directions

SLOW

1. Using a stand mixer on medium-high, cream the butter and sugar together until light in color. Add eggs and mix well.
2. Continue mixing on medium speed and slowly add the dry ingredients.
3. Add mashed ripe bananas and fold into the batter. Stir in any other mix-ins, if desired.
4. Grease a round slow cooker insert with butter. Pour in batter.
5. Cover the cooker with a paper towel, keeping it in place with the lid. This will collect condensation and keep your bread from getting soggy.
6. Cover and cook on HIGH for 2 to 3 hours (or until bread is done).

FAST

1. Mix dry ingredients and set aside.
2. Cream the butter and sugar together until light in color. Add eggs and mix well.
3. Continue mixing on medium speed and slowly add dry ingredients to the butter mixture. Add mashed ripe bananas and fold into the batter. Stir in any mix-ins, if desired.
4. Grease a small loaf pan that fits inside the Crock-Pot® Express.
5. Place a trivet inside the Crock-Pot® Express and then pour 1 c. water inside. Pour batter into the bread pan and cover with a paper towel. Tightly wrap the pan in foil and place on top of trivet.
6. Cover with the lid and close steam vent. Cook on Multigrain setting for 50 minutes followed by a quick release.
7. Remove bread and allow to cool on a wire rack before cutting.

Carrot Cake

Fluffy with a finger-licking good frosting, this dessert will be gone before you know it!

YIELD 8 portions **I SLOW COOK TIME** 3 to 4 hours **I EXPRESS COOK TIME** 50 minutes

Ingredients

- ⅔ c. flour
- ½ c. sugar
- 1 t. baking soda
- ¾ t. baking powder
- 1 t. ground cinnamon
- ¼ t. ground nutmeg
- 1 t. freshly grated ginger
- ¼ t. salt
- ⅓ c. vegetable oil
- 2 eggs
- 1 (8-oz.) can crushed pineapple with juice
- ½ c. golden raisins
- 1 c. pecans or walnuts, chopped (optional)
- 1 c. finely grated carrot

CREAM CHEESE FROSTING

- 4 oz. cream cheese, softened
- 1 c. powdered sugar
- ½ t. vanilla extract
  Sprinkles for decoration

NOTE Add 1 c. flaked coconut for Crock-Pot® Express.

Directions

SLOW

1. In a bowl combine flour, sugar, baking soda, baking powder, spices, ginger and salt. Stir with a whisk to mix well.
2. In another bowl combine vegetable oil, eggs, pineapple, raisins, nuts (if using) and carrot. Stir with a whisk to mix well.
3. Add the dry ingredients to the wet ingredients and mix by hand until everything is well incorporated.
4. Line a slow cooker with parchment paper, using enough to allow yourself to later remove the cake by lifting out the parchment. Pour cake batter into prepared cooker.
5. Cover the top of the cooker with 4 paper towels or a thin kitchen towel, making sure the towel is not touching the cake in the cooker. (This will prevent condensation from dripping on the cake.)
6. Cover with the lid and cook on HIGH for 3 to 4 hours. (A toothpick inserted into the center of the cake should come out clean.)
7. Remove the cake from the cook cooker and cool on a wire cooling rack for 5 minutes. Let cool completely before frosting.

FAST

1. Place a trivet in the Crock-Pot® Express and pour in 1 c. water.
2. Mix the dry ingredients in a small bowl: flour, sugar, baking soda, baking powder, spices and salt.
3. In another bowl, whisk eggs. Slowly add in oil. Stir in pineapple, coconut, raisins, carrots and nuts. Slowly add the dry ingredients to the wet ingredients and mix just until combined.
4. Grease a 6-in. springform pan (or other baking dish that fits into the Crock-Pot® Express).
5. Pour batter into the pan then cover with paper towel and wrap with foil. Place the pan on top of the trivet on the cooker.
6. Cover with the lid and close steam vent. Cook on Multigrain setting for 50 minutes followed by a quick release.
7. Remove the cake pan and cool cake on a wire cooling rack for 5 minutes.
8. Prepare icing while the cake is cooling. Ice once the cake is completely cooked. Enjoy!

Desserts

Caramelized Pineapples

This tropical dessert is perfectly sweet—try it next time it's too hot to turn on the oven!

YIELD 6 to 8 portions **I SLOW COOK TIME** 1 hour 30 minutes **I EXPRESS COOK TIME** 10 minutes

Ingredients

- 1 pineapple, peeled and sliced into rings.
- ½ c. white sugar, plus more to taste
- 3 T. unsalted butter
  Coconut ice cream, for serving

Directions

SLOW

1. Butter the bottom of the slow cooker. Cut remaining butter into small chunks and scatter over bottom of cooker.
2. Sprinkle sugar to coat the bottom of the cooker.
3. Top with a single layer of pineapple rings and then sprinkle with more sugar, if desired.
4. Cover and cook on HIGH for 1 hour 30 minutes.
5. Plate each pineapple ring then top with a scoop of coconut ice cream.

FAST

1. Set Crock-Pot® Express to Sauté and heat butter
2. Once butter is melted, sprinkle sugar to coat the bottom of the cooker.
3. Top with a single layer of pineapple rings.
4. Cook until pineapples start to caramelize, about 5 minutes, then flip.
5. Continue cooking until the pineapples are caramelized on both sides, about 5 more minutes.
6. Plate each pineapple ring then top with a scoop of coconut ice cream.

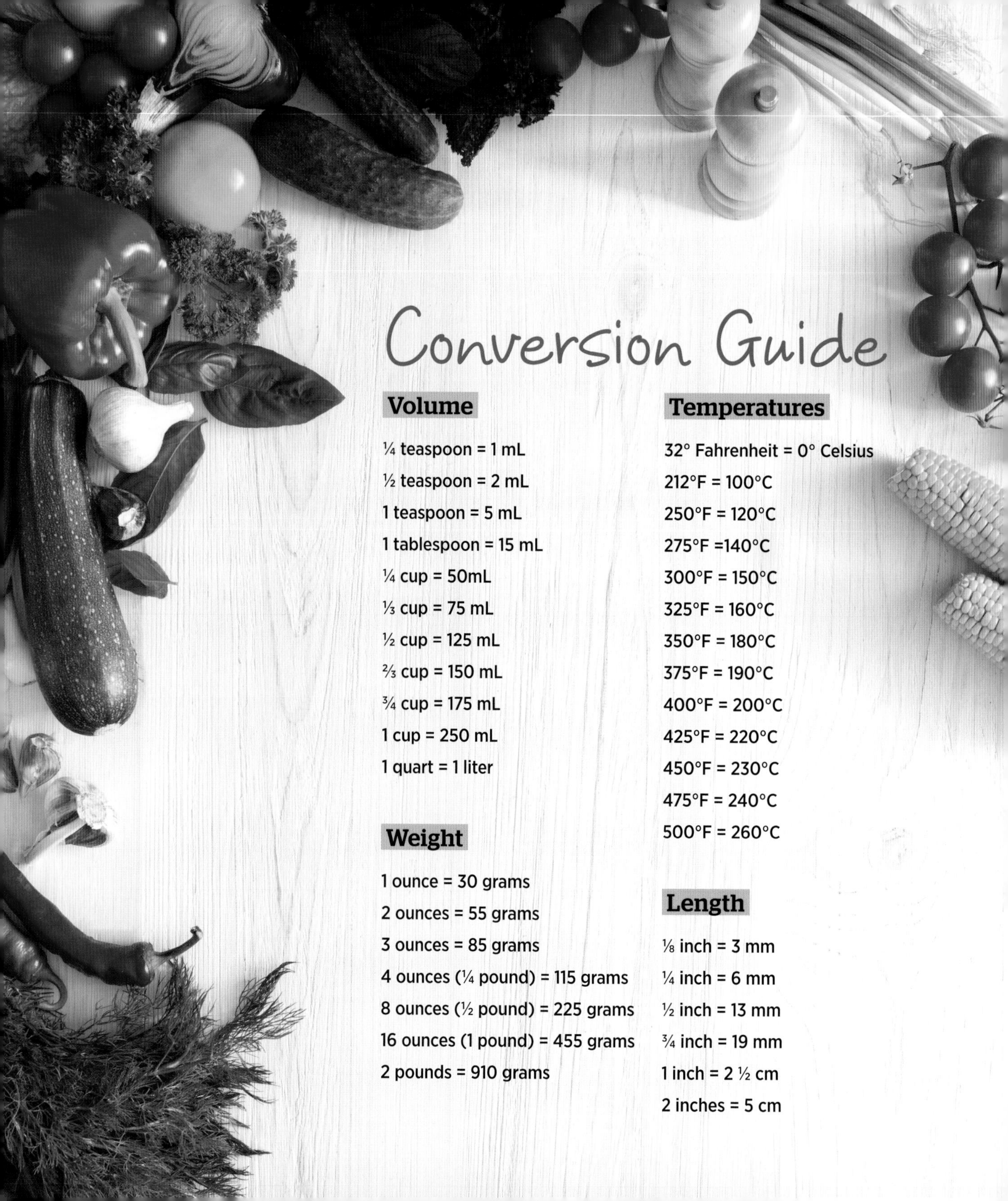

Conversion Guide

Volume

¼ teaspoon = 1 mL

½ teaspoon = 2 mL

1 teaspoon = 5 mL

1 tablespoon = 15 mL

¼ cup = 50mL

⅓ cup = 75 mL

½ cup = 125 mL

⅔ cup = 150 mL

¾ cup = 175 mL

1 cup = 250 mL

1 quart = 1 liter

Weight

1 ounce = 30 grams

2 ounces = 55 grams

3 ounces = 85 grams

4 ounces (¼ pound) = 115 grams

8 ounces (½ pound) = 225 grams

16 ounces (1 pound) = 455 grams

2 pounds = 910 grams

Temperatures

32° Fahrenheit = 0° Celsius

212°F = 100°C

250°F = 120°C

275°F =140°C

300°F = 150°C

325°F = 160°C

350°F = 180°C

375°F = 190°C

400°F = 200°C

425°F = 220°C

450°F = 230°C

475°F = 240°C

500°F = 260°C

Length

⅛ inch = 3 mm

¼ inch = 6 mm

½ inch = 13 mm

¾ inch = 19 mm

1 inch = 2 ½ cm

2 inches = 5 cm

Media Lab Books
For inquiries, call 646-838-6637

Copyright 2018 Topix Media Lab

Published by Topix Media Lab
14 Wall Street, Suite 4B
New York, NY 10005

Printed in China

ISBN-10: 1-942556-94-2
ISBN-13: 978-1-942556-94-7

Indexing by R studio T, NYC

Special Thanks: Marsha Bare, Rachel Garmers, Jessica Pethtel

Cover, Back Cover and all interior images Shutterstock except: all headshots of Jenn and p28, 45, 107, 108, 111, 123, 156 Courtesy Jenn Bare; p4 Milena Milani/Stocksy; p8 Eising Studio/Stockfood; p10 Jennifer_Sharp/iStock; p15 Pressbrake/iStock; p16 Jennifer_Sharp/iStock; p23 Milena Milani/stocksy; p24 Nadezhda Rybalchenko/Alamy; p58 Pinkybird/iStock; p71 margouillatphotos/iStock; p76 nata_vkusidey/iStock; p79 LauriPatterson/iStock; p84 grandriver/iStock; p87 boblin/iStock; p99 GMVozd/iStock; p131 LauriPatterson/iStock; p144 wsmahar/iStock; p151 NightAndDayImages/iStock; p159 Christopher Gould/Stockfood; p176 travellinglight/iStock; p187 Jeff Wasserman/Stocksy; p218 JJAVA/Adobe Stock; p228 LauriPatterson/iStock; p233 iuliia_n/iStock; p243 chas53/iStock.

Index

Mushroom Wild Rice pg. 101